The Louisiana Purchase

TURNINGPOINTS

Preeminent writers offering fresh, personal
perspectives on the defining events of our time

Published Titles

William Least Heat-Moon, *Columbus in the Americas*

Scott Simon, *Jackie Robinson and
the Integration of Baseball*

Alan Dershowitz, *America Declares Independence*

Thomas Fleming, *The Louisiana Purchase*

Forthcoming Titles

Douglas Brinkley on the March on Washington

William F. Buckley Jr. on the Fall of the Berlin Wall

Eleanor Clift on Passing the 19th Amendment

Sir Martin Gilbert on D-Day

Martin Goldsmith on the Beatles Coming to America

TURNING POINTS

The Louisiana Purchase

THOMAS FLEMING

WILEY

John Wiley & Sons, Inc.

Published by John Wiley & Sons, Inc., Hoboken, New Jersey
Published simultaneously in Canada

Design and production by Navta Associates, Inc.

For general information about our other products and services, please contact our Customer Care Department within the United States at (800) 762-2974, outside the United States at (317) 572-3993 or fax (317) 572-4002.

Wiley also publishes its books in a variety of electronic formats. Some content that appears in print may not be available in electronic books. For more information about Wiley products, visit our web site www.wiley.com.

Library of Congress Cataloging-in-Publication Data:

Fleming, Thomas J.
    The Louisiana Purchase / Thomas Fleming.
        p. cm. — (Turning points)
    ISBN 0-471-26738-4 (Cloth)
    1. Louisiana Purchase. I. Title. II. Turning points (John Wiley & Sons)
    E333 .F56 2003
    973.4'6—dc21
                                                            2002156131
Printed in the United States of America

10 9 8 7 6 5 4 3 2 1

Contents

1

Idealist at Work

The greatest diplomatic triumph in the history of the United States began with a blunder. In July 1801, four months after Thomas Jefferson took over the "presidential palace," as the unfinished White House was then called, Louis Andre Pichon, the affable young chargé d'affaires of the French Republic, visited the United States' new chief executive. That such a low-ranking diplomat was France's sole spokesman in the new U.S. capital was stark evidence of the strained relations between the world's only two republics. Normally an ambassador would be on hand to handle such an important relationship.

From 1798 to 1800, France and the United States had fought a vicious, undeclared war at sea in which French privateers and frigates had despoiled a staggering $12 million in U.S. ships and cargoes (the modern equivalent of almost $200 million). American men-of-war had slugged it out ship to ship with many of these depredators. Fearful of a French invasion, George Washington had emerged from retirement to head a ten thousand–man

U.S. army, and appointed General Alexander Hamilton as its field commander.

The war had emerged as a byproduct of the larger war France was waging with England. The French were furiously resentful over what they considered American treachery—the United States' refusal to honor the treaty of alliance it had signed with King Louis XVI in 1778, which had enabled the new republic to win independence from England.

President George Washington had declared the United States neutral in the struggle that erupted between Revolutionary France and England in 1793. He had decided that the French Republic, having beheaded Louis XVI, was no longer the same country with whom the United States had been allied during its revolution. France—and numerous French partisans in the United States—thought there was a distinctly pro-English tilt to this international balancing act. Washington's successor, President John Adams, partly agreed with this view, and had sent three commissioners to Europe to negotiate an end to the so-called Quasi-War.

Louis Andre Pichon had acted as secretary of the French delegation to this parley and played a major role in working out an agreement that called for a "firm, inviolable and universal peace." But many skeptical Americans, notably members of the Federalist Party led by Jefferson's chief rival, General Alexander Hamilton, still nursed violently antagonistic feelings toward France. They found special grounds for complaint about this treaty, in which the United States had abandoned millions of dollars in claims by U.S. merchants for losses in the Quasi-War. In return, France agreed to release the United States from the Treaty of 1778, which the Federalists considered already defunct.

Thomas Jefferson was not one of these Francophobes. On the contrary, the tall, red haired, freckle-faced president greeted Pichon warmly as the spokesman for a country that stirred his deepest political emotions. For the previous nine years, Jefferson had defended the French Revolution against fierce criticism in the United States. Even when France collapsed into an orgy of mob rule and raw terror in 1793–1794, Jefferson retained his faith in the revolution's redeeming value. Repeatedly he had insisted that "the liberty of the whole earth" depended on a French victory against England and the other European powers that had assailed France after Louis XVI's execution. Rather than permit "this cause" to fail, Jefferson told one friend, he "would have seen half the earth desolated."

Jefferson's followers, who soon coalesced into the Republican Party, often expressed this vehement opinion in riotous demonstrations in the streets of New York and other cities. President Washington viewed these numerous, so-called Democratic Societies as seedbeds of insurrection. Their behavior, combined with the far worse excesses of the French Revolution, convinced conservatives that liberty and equality were dangerous ideas. This conviction became part of the Federalist Party's gospel.

Pichon was hoping for a demonstration of Jefferson's friendship for France. The young chargé asked the president about U.S. policy toward the troubled island of Santo Domingo. Then, as now, it was divided into a French-speaking western third (the future republic of Haiti) and a Spanish-speaking eastern two thirds (the future Dominican Republic) with a range of mountains as a geographical barrier between them. Spain had ceded the Spanish part of the island to France in 1795. The French section's sugar, coffee, and indigo plantations once made it France's most valuable overseas possession. The French Revolution had triggered a civil war that wrecked the economy.

Out of the turmoil emerged an extraordinary black leader, Toussaint L'Ouverture, who ruled both enclaves, in which some four hundred thousand ex-slaves lived uneasily with thousands of whites and free mulattoes. Toussaint was immensely proud of his martial prowess and did not complain when his followers called him "the Bonaparte of the Antilles."

Pichon, who spoke excellent English, asked Jefferson what the United States would do if France tried to regain control of Santo Domingo. Would it support such an effort? A smiling Jefferson replied that "nothing would be easier than to supply everything for your army and navy, and to starve out Toussaint."

This was a startling reversal of the policy of President John Adams, who had seen L'Ouverture's emergence as an opportunity to frustrate British and French imperialism in the Caribbean. Adams and his secretary of state, Timothy Pickering, had shipped L'Ouverture's army food and ammunition, which helped them defeat a British army that attempted to seize Santo Domingo. They also sent Edward Stevens, an old friend of Alexander Hamilton, to the island's major port, Cap Francois, where he became

L'Ouverture's trusted friend and adviser and urged him to declare independence.

Jefferson assured Pichon that most Americans had no enthusiasm for an independent Santo Domingo ruled by a black dictator, who was a walking, talking threat to the peace and prosperity of every American state with large numbers of slaves. In September 1800, Virginia had been badly shaken by an aborted rebellion led by two free Africans, Gabriel Prosser, a Richmond blacksmith, and his brother Martin, an itinerant preacher.

Jefferson also told Pichon he thought it was likely that an isolated Toussaint would turn to piracy to finance his rule. There was a grave danger of Santo Domingo becoming "an Algiers in American waters." In the Mediterranean, the Moslems of Algiers and other North African cities regularly preyed upon merchant ships of all nations. Jefferson grandly predicted that if rumors of an early peace between France and England were true, the British would join in a campaign to remove Toussaint from the political scene and reimpose white control on Santo Domingo. England also had islands in the West Indies that were crowded with slaves made restless by the French Revolution's cry of liberty, equality, and fraternity.

A delighted Pichon rushed back to his residence and reported the president's statement to his superior in Paris, Foreign Minister Charles Maurice de Talleyrand-Perigord, one of the most corrupt and devious politicians in the history of France or any other nation. Talleyrand was born into a noble family that traced their pedigree to the year 1000. He was pressured by his father into becoming a priest because a boyhood injury had left him with a serious limp. On the eve of the French Revolution, his father secured him the bishopric of Autun—a favor he soon regretted. The son, already notorious for his impiety, sided with the revolutionists and was soon excommunicated by the pope.

When Talleyrand took charge of the foreign office in 1797, he had reportedly exulted: "I am going to make an immense fortune!" One of his first moves was a demand for a huge bribe from American diplomats to settle the growing tensions between the United States and France. The Americans had reacted with public indignation, replying: "No, not a sixpence!" In subsequent telling, this became a fervid slogan: "Millions for defense, but not one cent for tribute." The undeclared war soon followed.

The episode deepened Talleyrand's already low opinion of Americans. In the mid-1790s, he had spent two years in the United States escaping the revolution's reign of terror and departed with the fixed opinion that these newcomers to the family of nations were boring, self-righteous upstarts who needed to be put in their place. One of the best ways to do this, Talleyrand had concluded, was to check their westward expansion by gaining control of Florida and the Mississippi River basin, establishing "a wall of brass" that the Americans could never penetrate, even if they called on the British for help.

Pichon's dispatch was soon being pondered by the man who had brought order out of the chaos of the French Revolution—First Consul Napoleon Bonaparte. Born into a family of petty, largely penniless Corsican aristocrats two years after France purchased the island from Genoa in 1767, Napoleon was educated at elite French military schools. He managed to qualify for a career in the royal army in spite of speaking French with a heavy Corsican accent. The 1789 revolution levitated this strong-willed soldier to ever-increasing power, thanks to his ability to organize and lead men, his readiness to take risks and his utter ruthlessness. The upheaval also instilled in him a carefully concealed loathing for the masses and their violent tendencies.

By the age of twenty-five, Bonaparte was a brigadier general and a man to watch. Seven years later, on November 10, 1799, he led a coup d'etat that made him one of three consuls entrusted with executive power. Bonaparte was the only consul that mattered. Under a new constitution, the legislature was an easily manipulated three-tiered affair—a senate that introduced Bonaparte's decrees, a tribunate that debated them, and an assembly that voted their approval. Announcing that the "romance of the revolution" was over, Napoleon imprisoned or exiled radicals and ruled as a civilian, with more authority than Louis XVI ever dreamed of wielding.

The British, exhausted and almost bankrupt after nine years of global war, were ready to sign a peace treaty, leaving this military genius the virtual ruler of Europe. At the Battle of Marengo in 1800, Napoleon had smashed the army of England's chief ally, Austria, and forced Vienna to sign a humiliating peace in February 1801, in which it surrendered the Grand Duchy of Tuscany.

"The Man of Destiny," as millions of admirers called

Bonaparte, welcomed President Jefferson's invitation to retake Santo Domingo. The conquest of the island was a first step in Napoleon's plan to reestablish France's empire in North America, which it had lost in the Seven Years' War (1754–1761) with England and her continental allies. Talleyrand, the man who had given Napoleon the idea, was equally pleased. It is easy to imagine these two cynics exchanging smiles. The naivete of these Americans! They still thought that the ideals of the French Revolution were alive and meaningful in France. Napoleon—and the artful Talleyrand—knew that only one reality mattered now: power.

If all went well, Talleyrand's vision of French control of the Mississippi River valley would achieve glorious fruition on Napoleon's bayonets. Jefferson and his government would become another French satellite, like Belgium, the Netherlands, Switzerland, and the petty kingdoms of Germany and Italy. The First Consul would rule not only Europe but also North America. Control of South America would inevitably follow. King Carlos IV of Spain was already terrified of Napoleon's power. Finally, with the gold and silver of the mines of Mexico and Peru, and the bountiful harvests and enterprising seamen of the United States at France's command, the Man of Destiny would turn on England and crush that nation of conniving shopkeepers once and for all.

The supposed peace between the United States and France was called the Treaty of Mortefontaine, named after the country chateau owned by Bonaparte's older brother, Joseph, where it had been signed. The agreement had been followed the next day by a very different treaty in Spain. The chief negotiator was Lucien Bonaparte, younger brother of the First Consul. Signed at San Ildefonso, a country palace of the Spanish king, this treaty stipulated that Spain would return to France the immense territory of Louisiana, which King Louis XV had given to Spain in 1763 to compensate his Iberian ally for its losses in their struggle with England in the Seven Years' War. In return, Napoleon would place the son-in-law of the Spanish king on the throne of the Duchy of Tuscany and name him monarch of a new kingdom called Etruria. To prove that this was a transaction between firm friends, the First Consul pledged never to cede Louisiana to a third power, for any reason.

It would be hard to imagine a more graphic demonstration of the cynicism of the Talleyrand-Bonaparte team. Within twenty-four hours they solemnly vowed to renew their friendship with the United States at Mortefontaine and cut a deal at San Ildefonso that they knew would rupture this friendship the moment the news got out. Of course, they were presuming that the news would not get out until they were ready to let it out.

What was the territory of Louisiana? Nothing less than the heart of the American continent. It stretched from the Canadian border to the mouth of the Mississippi, and from the western bank of the great river to "the Shining Mountains," the Indian name for the Rockies. As a vital adjunct to this vast "retrocession," Napoleon also wanted the Spanish colonies of East and West Florida, which comprised the present-day state of Florida, plus portions of what is now the state of Louisiana on the east bank of the Mississippi up to the thirtieth parallel of latitude. This swatch of the continent had four hundred miles of coastline along which France could create naval bases that would dominate the waters of the Caribbean and the Gulf of Mexico. Bonaparte ordered Talleyrand to begin bargaining with the Spanish king to add this final touch to his vision of restored colonial power.

Santo Domingo fit into this ambitious scheme as a source of badly needed cash. Napoleon was convinced that the island could again become the cornucopia it had been before the French Revolution. Instead of buying food from the Americans, the way the colony had previously operated, the victuals would now come at bargain prices from French farms in Louisiana. First, however, Toussaint L'Ouverture and his fellow generals—"these gilded Africans" as Bonaparte called them—would have to be eliminated.

While signing preliminary articles of peace with the English in October 1801, Bonaparte obtained their approval to send an expedition to regain Santo Domingo. To bolster his argument, he paraphrased President Jefferson's fears that Toussaint L'Ouverture would turn to piracy. Bonaparte promptly ordered his brother-in-law, aggressive General Charles Leclerc, and twenty thousand of France's best troops to prepare to depart for the Caribbean. So confident was the first consul of swift success, he saw no reason why his beautiful younger sister, Pauline, should not accompany her handsome husband.

The First Consul commanded Leclerc to subdue and

occupy Santo Domingo—a task Bonaparte estimated would require no more than six weeks—and then detach a large portion of his army to take possession of Louisiana. Included in Leclerc's orders was the commitment that clever Chargé Pichon had extracted at the White House: "Jefferson has promised that the instant the French army arrives, all measures will be taken to starve Toussaint and to aid the army."

2

Realist at Work

In Washington, D.C., Secretary of State James Madison presided over a handful of clerks in a square brick building down the street from the White House. The tiny Department of State shared the structure with the equally minuscule Department of War. On the other side of the White House a similar brick building housed the slightly larger Treasury Department. In the new capital, the entire federal government, including members of Congress and the Supreme Court, numbered only 293 people.

In 1801 the State Department was the "ear" through which the country listened to confidential reports on what was happening in the rest of the world. As the year lengthened, Secretary of State Madison did not like what he was hearing. Rumors were swirling through Europe about Spain "retroceding" Louisiana to France. The secret treaty of San Idelfonso was growing less secret with every passing day.

A climax of sorts was a letter from Rufus King, the U.S. minister to England, stating that "in all probability" Spain had ceded Louisiana and the Floridas to France. Even more worrisome was another part of King's letter, in which he reported that "certain influential persons in France" thought that "nature has marked a line of separation between the people of the United States living upon the two sides of the range of mountains that divides their territory." This produced the specter of French money and ideology being used to seduce western Americans to secede from the union and form a separate nation west of the Appalachian Mountains.

Around the same time, Virginian Fulwar Skipwith, the new commercial agent for the United States in Paris, wrote Jefferson that "certain men in high office" had "industriously circulated" a report that Louisiana was to remain Spanish property. Skipwith said he was "sure of the reverse." An old Paris hand—he had previously been consul general—Skipwith had also learned that the French government had formed a plan of "peopling that country to an amazing extent."

Secretary of State Madison decided it was time to have a talk with Chargé d'Affaires Pichon. The tone would be very different from the promise of perpetual friendship with France that Jefferson had delivered in July.

The contrast between the tall, ebullient U.S. president and the small, severely self-controlled Madison was at first glance almost puzzling. Seemingly total opposites, they were extremely close friends. Only a few people knew how much Jefferson depended on Madison's cool analytic mind to ballast his often soaring enthusiasms.

Madison recognized the importance of Jefferson's

visionary gifts, which enabled him to make the 1776 declaration of independence a document that transformed a
colonial revolt into a struggle with global spiritual over-
tones. Jefferson in turn recognized the power of Madison's
intellect, which had enabled him to create almost single-
handedly the federal constitution that rescued the United
States from disorder and disunion in 1787.

Even more important was Madison's ability to deal with
Jefferson's impulsive and erratic style without impairing
their friendship. In his later years, Madison often said that
"allowances ought to be made" for the Jeffersonian tendency to express "in strong and round terms the impressions of the moment."

Madison's talk with Chargé Pichon swiftly became a
demonstration of his readiness to correct the impression
that the United States was prepared to be France's unques-
tioning partner in Bonaparte's plan to regain control of
Santo Domingo. "Summoning up the most circumspect
and studied expression he could," Pichon nervously related
in his subsequent dispatch, the secretary asked if the
report of Louisiana's retrocession was true. Madison
hoped it was an idea that had occurred to French strate-
gists during the "late naval war" and had been abandoned
once peace between the two countries had been confirmed. French ownership of the west bank of the Mississippi and the port of New Orleans, through which western
Americans exported tons of grain, cotton, and other farm
products, was certain to lead to "collisions" that would
endanger the peace between the two nations.

The agitated Pichon claimed to know nothing about the

rumor of France obtaining Louisiana. But he admitted that several times since their revolution, various French leaders had talked of regaining the territory. Surely Madison did not imply that was a crime?

Not at all, Madison smoothly replied. But he still thought it would be a political mistake. Spain, the present owner of the territory, was "peaceable." The Americans were accustomed to the Spanish, who had some odd quirks, but permitted them to use the river and the port of New Orleans under the terms of a treaty that the Washington administration had negotiated with Madrid in 1795. The French would introduce a new element in that political equation. At the same time, Madison said he did not want Pichon to think that the United States was in any way worried about French troops in Louisiana. The amazing growth of the western population had eliminated the country's concerns on that score.

Did Madison's talk of collisions mean the Americans were getting ready to go beyond the Mississippi? Pichon asked.

Of course not, Madison replied. He dismissed the idea as a "chimera." But the jittery French diplomat was by no means convinced of this disavowal, which might mean no more than his own claim to know nothing about France's repossession of Louisiana.

Once more Pichon tried to calm the secretary's fears. Europeans shared the use of many rivers without undue friction. Why couldn't the two republics negotiate any and all points of contention? Madison shook his head and repeated his prediction that France in Louisiana meant "collisions."

Back in his residence, Pichon wrote a dispatch to Paris that more than demonstrated how effectively Madison had worked on him. The chargé warned Talleyrand that the plan to transfer Louisiana to France might mean a war that would bring England into the conflict as a U.S ally. If the first consul proceeded with his program, it would be vital to select with the utmost care the officials who came to Louisiana. Almost as if he were trying to prove Madison's point that the Americans were formidable, Pichon noted that the population of the new state of Kentucky had leaped from sixty thousand to two hundred fifty thousand in fifteen years.

Growth was undoubtedly the American republic's out-standing characteristic, especially in the West. Between 1750 and 1800, the overall U.S. population rose from 1,170,000 to 5 million. Between 1790 and 1800, the population of the first two western states, Kentucky and Tennessee, rose 300 percent. Kentucky had more people than five of the original states (New Hampshire, Rhode Island, New Jersey, Delaware, and Georgia). Growing almost as fast was the territory of Ohio, which would soon become the seventeenth state.

Beneath this facade of vigor were disturbing tensions. The people of the western waters, as they liked to style themselves, had a heady sense of a separate democratic des-tiny that at times verged on downright dislike of the sup-posedly arrogant and conservative East. In 1794, when the U.S. Congress attempted to raise money by imposing taxes on whiskey that Westerners distilled from their grain, the citizens in and around Pittsburgh, Pennsylvania, rose in revolt, terrorized federal tax collectors, and talked of setting up a separate nation. Similar voices were heard in the western valleys of Virginia and the Carolinas.

President George Washington, urged on by his pugnacious Secretary of the Treasury, Alexander Hamilton, had raised an army and smashed this "Whiskey Rebellion" without firing a shot. But worries about the West's loyalty to the federal union continued to trouble more than one thoughtful American, as Rufus King's letter to Madison made clear.

In 1801, lingering suspicions of similar disloyalty still swirled around the commander of the U.S. Army, General James Wilkinson, who had been a staff officer in the American Revolution. Moving to Kentucky after the war, he went into land speculation and politics. In 1788 he led a campaign for Kentucky's independence, claiming for himself a dubious expertise in dealing with the Spanish in New Orleans. The new federal government persuaded most Kentuckians to choose statehood within the union.

By that time, Wilkinson was so cozy with the governor of Louisiana that he swore a covert allegiance to the Spanish crown and became Agent 13 in their secret service, receiving a stipend of $2,000 a year. Rejoining the regular U.S. Army, he rose swiftly to brigadier general and in 1797 became commander in chief—a job to which President Jefferson reappointed him, dismissing rumors of his divided allegiance.

Thomas Jefferson's transfer of the government to Washington, D.C., was an arrangement he had worked out in a negotiation with Alexander Hamilton when they were both in Washington's cabinet. It had not endeared him to his Federalist critics, who tended to live in cities and towns and pursue commercial careers. But Jefferson's largely rural followers saw nothing wrong with the raw "federal village" in which the government began operating in 1800. They liked the president's casual style—his habit of receiving visitors in old clothes and carpet slippers or jumping on a horse to do his own shopping. They saw nothing wrong with the "common" post and rail fence he had built around the White House. All this was in keeping with what Jefferson called "Republican simplicity."

Unfortunately, the rest of the country was growing in ways that made Republican simplicity seem more affectation than reality. With the 1793 invention of the cotton gin, Eli Whitney had opened the door to fortunes for Southern planters. Now Whitney was manufacturing guns in New Haven using interchangeable parts—a first step to mass production. Textile factories were sprouting in other parts of New England. Four out of five Americans still made their living as farmers, but they were doing far more than feeding themselves and their families. They were exporting tons of wheat, corn, and cotton for handsome profits.

Between 1793 and 1801, U.S. export sales quintupled to $70 million a year, and most of the goods and produce were carried in U.S. ships. When the federal government under James Madison's constitution went into operation in 1789 there were only three banks in the country. By 1801, there were twenty-nine banks and their capital had multiplied six-fold. Moreover, U.S. bankers were in regular communication with the great merchant bankers of Europe, giving them vastly expanded sources of credit.

Thanks to the financial system established by Alexander Hamilton when he was secretary of the treasury under George Washington, the United States had the highest credit rating in the world. The nation's net worth was estimated to be $1.8 billion. No less than three hundred printers turned out newspapers for a reading public that had practically eliminated illiteracy. Booksellers had multiplied fifty times since the end of the Revolution in 1783. The population of U.S.cities such as New York, Boston, and Philadelphia was growing almost as rapidly as the states of the West.

The affluent East thought Washington, D.C., was a prime example of the extremism—and hypocrisy—of Republican simplicity. In his unfinished White House, President Jefferson presided over a wine cellar stocked with expensive European vintages. The president's mountaintop mansion, Monticello, in Virginia, was neither simple nor rustic. Then there was the unfinished capitol a mile down muddy Pennsylvania Avenue from the White House. Because Jefferson had abolished most of the taxes levied by his predecessors, the U.S. Treasury lacked the cash to erect the central hall and dome. The two wings were connected by a crude wooden walkway.

Although Jefferson's Republican Party had dominating majorities in both houses of Congress, his rule was not as secure as it looked to a casual observer. There were some alarming fissures in the self-styled party of the people. On the left wing were "Old Republicans," ideologues who were in many cases committed to an almost paranoid fear of the federal government's power and an even more paranoid dislike of the Federalists, who had taken the name of their party from their belief in the beneficent effects of federal authority.

The Old Republicans wanted to sweep out every Federalist officeholder in the nation, from the lowliest postmaster to the clerks of the executive departments in Washington, D.C. They were not thrilled when Jefferson had tried to heal the breach between the two parties by declaring in his inaugural address, "We are all republicans, we are all federalists." They were even less enthused by his retention of Federalists in many government jobs.

These policies were heartily approved by another wing of the party, sometimes called "National Republicans." Chief among these was Secretary of State Madison, who had worked closely with Alexander Hamilton to set up the new federal government that the Constitution had created. Secretary of the Treasury Albert Gallatin, who had taken over Hamilton's financial system with scarcely a change, was another of these middle-of-the-road Republicans who urged Jefferson to shun the fanaticism of the Old Republicans and lure moderate Federalists into their party.

Still another political fissure, less concerned with ideology, revolved around the enigmatic figure of Jefferson's vice president, Aaron Burr of New York. An astute politician, Burr had carried his home state for the Republicans and made Thomas Jefferson president. But when the two men became deadlocked in the electoral college, Burr, in the view of many Republicans, had behaved treacherously by allegedly flirting with a Federalist offer to make him president in Jefferson's place. Burr steadfastly denied this slur, and there is little objective evidence to support it. But the president, listening to Burr's numerous Republican enemies in New York, became convinced of its truth, and the vice president slowly discovered he was persona non grata at the White House.

For the time being, Louisiana relegated worries about Old Republicans and Burr to the sidelines. Dissatisfied with Chargé Pichon's answers, President Jefferson and Secretary of State Madison decided it was time to send a minister plenipotentiary to Paris who could find out the truth about Louisiana. Their choice was a man who at first glance had little in common with Republican simplicity. Robert R. Livingston of New York was as wealthy in land and as confident in his lineage as any European aristocrat. In the Hudson River Valley, he presided over thousands of acres of farms and tenants.

Livingston's great-grandfather had emigrated from Scotland in 1672 and, by dint of hard dealing in the fur trade and in the politics of the colony of New York, acquired 160,000 acres and the "Lordship" of the "Manor of Livingston." By the time his great-grandson became minister to France in 1801, the manor had added many thousands of additional acres on both sides of the Hudson, and the Livingston family virtually assumed that it was their destiny to play major roles in their country's politics.

In spite of his wealth, Robert Livingston had backed the American Revolution and served ably in the Continental Congress as a delegate from New York. Toward the end of the eight-year struggle for independence, Livingston had become the Foreign Secretary of Congress, making him a kind of secretary of state in embryo. The experience left him with few illusions about the way Europeans practiced diplomacy—a background that undoubtedly had not a little to do with why Jefferson and Madison chose him as the minister to Paris. Another by no means unimportant factor was Livingston's enduring friendship with France, rooted in his personal knowledge of how crucial French aid was in winning the war for independence. Finally there was Jefferson's estimate of him as a man with a mind of "the first order."

Livingston's only flaw was a growing deafness. But there is little evidence that it interfered with his diplomatic performance. Madison and Jefferson instructed the New York manor lord to find out if there was any truth to the rumor that Louisiana was about to become French, and, if true, ordered him to do everything in his power to dissuade Napoleon from the transfer. But he was also told "to do nothing that would unnecessarily irritate our future neighbors, or check the liberality which they may be disposed to exercise in relation to the trade and navigation through the mouth of the Mississippi." At this point, the fall of 1801, Jefferson was still loath to abandon his dream of a happy partnership with France.

The new minister plenipotentiary set out for France on October 15, 1801, traveling in his usual aristocratic style. His wife, his two daughters and their husbands, numerous servants, and the secretary of the legation, Thomas

Sumter, crowded aboard the frigate *USS Boston*. Livingston's splendid coach was lashed to the open deck and served as a parlor for the ladies. They survived a sea voyage that included an all-too-common episode of terror. Off the French coast, waves towered above the quarterdeck and a violent wind seemed certain to drive them onto the rocky shore. But the wind suddenly shifted and the *Boston* struggled into the port of L'Orient.

By December 3, the Livingstons were in Paris, where they were welcomed by Fulwar Skipwith and other members of the U.S. colony. Even warmer was the greeting of the minister's old friend from revolutionary days, the Marquis de Lafayette. Fleeing the French Revolution's reign of terror, the marquis had sought refuge with the Austrians. They blamed him for his role in the upheaval, and he spent much of the next decade in prison. Diplomatic pressure on the part of his U.S. friends had helped free him, and Napoleon had permitted him to return to France with the hope that he would support the first consul's regime.

Another warm greeter was suave François Barbe-Marbois, who had been secretary to the French legation in Philadelphia during the American Revolution. He had married an American woman and had worked closely with Livingston to keep the alliance of the two countries alive in spite of much criticism and disillusionment on both sides. Marbois also had been a victim of the French Revolution's turmoil. In 1797 he had been seized and exiled to the pestilential village of Sinammary in French Guyana.

His wife had a mental breakdown from which she never recovered. Napoleon, seeking to reconcile all classes and political creeds, had recalled the former royalist and made him France's minister of finance.

With the help of these two friends, Livingston quickly achieved official status. He was presented to Foreign Minister Talleyrand on December 5, and the next day made his initial bow to the ruler of France, First Consul Bonaparte. The introduction took place in the Hall of Ministers in the old royal palace of the Tuileries. Livingston was accompanied by his two sons-in-law wearing the uniforms of aide-de-camps to the governor of New York. After waiting for an hour, they were ushered to the Audience Room between parallel lines of magnificently uniformed consular guards. There the first consul, in a gorgeous red coat embroidered with gold, paced around a waiting circle of diplomats, exchanging a few words with each, while Foreign Secretary Talleyrand limped after him.

When Bonaparte reached Livingston in his diplomatic promenade, the first consul asked if he had been to Europe before. When Livingston said no, Bonaparte said: "You have come to a very corrupt world." Turning to Talleyrand, he brusquely added: "Explain to him that the old world is very corrupt. You know something about that, don't you?"

There is no record of Talleyrand's reply. No answer was required. The first consul and his chief adviser were mocking the U.S. minister and his naive president. The ex-bishop of Autun, as Livingston well knew, was the man whose greed for a bribe had plunged France and the United States into the Quasi-War. Here he stood, with his dead eyes and supercilious smile, exchanging jokes about corruption at the right hand of France's ruler. Fortunately, Livingston's self-esteem was too solid to worry about the possibility that he was being insulted. Instead, with a boldness that came naturally to this burly six-footer, he went to work on finding out what the French were planning to do with Louisiana.

3

The Game Begins

Two weeks after Napoleon's sardonic exchange with Robert Livingston in the Tuileries palace, General Leclerc and his fleet and army sailed from Brest. To smooth their arrival, Bonaparte dispatched a friendly letter to Toussaint L'Ouverture. "We have conceived esteem for you," he wrote. "And we take pleasure in proclaiming the great service you have rendered to the French people. What can you desire?—the liberty of the blacks? You know that in all the countries where we [the French] have been, we have given it to peoples who had it not."

Leclerc's armada hove to off the coast of Santo Domingo in late January 1802. By this time, Secretary of State Madison's policy diverged sharply from President Jefferson's burst of Francophile enthusiasm in July. A new U.S. consul, Tobias Lear, former private secretary to George Washington, had replaced Edward Stevens in Santo Domingo. One of his first statements when he arrived in Cap Francois was a fulsome congratulation of Toussaint L'Ouverture for his wise and benevolent rule of Santo Domingo.

When a troubled Louis Pichon protested this embrace of the black ruler, Madison smoothly assured him that he and Jefferson disapproved of Lear's statement. At the same time, he informed Pichon that the U.S. government thought it was important to retain the friendship of these ex-slave rulers—the blacks of Guadaloupe had recently risen in revolt—lest in revenge they try to excite U.S. slaves to rebel. Pichon hurried to the White House and reminded the president of his promise to starve Toussaint. To his dismay, Pichon found Jefferson "reserved and cold."

On Santo Domingo, the size of Leclerc's fleet and army made L'Ouverture and his allies more than a little suspicious. It was too large to be the mere escort of a delegation from Paris, reaffirming France's theoretical sovereignty over the island. When Leclerc called on Henri Christophe, one of L'Ouverture's generals, to surrender Cap Francois, Christophe declined. Leclerc promptly attacked from land and sea. Christophe responded by burning the port city and slaughtering the white inhabitants before retreating into the countryside.

An exasperated Leclerc found himself in a ruined city where almost all the food was in U.S. ships in the harbor and American-owned warehouses ashore. Relying on Jefferson's promise of collaboration, he tried to buy food from the Americans and was outraged by the prices they demanded. He rushed an agent to New York to borrow a million francs. Not a single bank in that city or in Philadelphia would lend him a cent. The disorders of the revolution had destroyed French credit around the world.

Grimly, Leclerc seized supplies from the Americans and

named his own prices. When U.S. ship captains and merchants protested, they were insulted and threatened with the seizure of their vessels. Soon U.S. newspapers were indignantly reporting the French general's high-handed behavior, which stirred unpleasant memories of the Quasi-War.

By the first week in March, Madison and Jefferson were hearing a first-person account of the turmoil on Santo Domingo. The report came from a U.S. ship captain who had witnessed the destruction of Cap Francois and risked his life to rescue some white inhabitants from General Christophe's vengeance. The captain brought with him a letter from Tobias Lear, adding additional details. Even more important was a letter from a Kentuckian who was serving as a captain in Leclerc's cavalry. This soldier of fortune informed Lear that a part of the French expedition was destined for Louisiana.

General Leclerc bombarded Chargé d'Affaires Pichon with letters, ordering him to make the United States deliver on their promise to feed his army. Pichon replied with a stream of advice and thinly disguised reprimands. Abusing U.S. ship captains and merchants was not the way to win American friendship. As for handing him the problem of supplying the army, Pichon boldly informed Talleyrand that it made no sense. Why did France send an army to Santo Domingo without money or advice on how to supply it? Someone in Paris was very close to incompetent.

When Pichon sought help from Secretary of State Madison, he found himself answering difficult questions: Why was the French army so large? Shouldn't Paris have explained the first consul's plans before the expedition sailed? He also mentioned the report from Tobias Lear that part of the army was destined for Louisiana. Was that true?

Pichon stoutly maintained that he had no information about French plans for Louisiana, which was true as far as it went. He asked Madison to cooperate with France by allowing him to publish a letter announcing that trade with Santo Domingo was henceforth limited to ports controlled by France. He hoped Madison would publish a statement in support of this policy.

Madison's answer was a masterpiece of evasion. He said it was very difficult to control the "national spirit" of a nation as commercially minded as the United States. The Southern states might support such an embargo because they feared the rebellious message L'Ouverture personified. But the Northern states, already rather hostile to the South, would violate it with impunity to sell their products to L'Ouverture's regime.

The chargé all but begged for a loan of at least a million francs. Madison stared at Pichon as if he had gone insane. A loan was out of the question, the secretary of state said. It would cause a huge uproar in Congress, which was extremely jittery about the ratification of the clause in the Treaty of Mortefontaine in which the United States abandoned the claims of U.S. merchants for their losses in the Quasi-War.

A desperate Pichon went to the White House and pleaded with Jefferson for a loan, implicitly reminding him of his promise to starve Toussaint. The chargé came away from this meeting with renewed hope. He told Foreign

Minister Talleyrand that the president had spoken to him "with the language of sincerity and marked interest." Jefferson promised to consult with members of Congress who were coming to one of his dinner parties "to consider what could be done."

Pichon's hopes soon plummeted. He heard nothing from Jefferson or Republican congressmen eager to help France. Instead, he was approached by a number of Federalist legislators who urged him to take a stronger stand against the Jefferson administration over the way they were treating Leclerc's army. Pichon had no trouble figuring out that these politicians were only trying to embarrass the president and his secretary of state.

Meanwhile, General Leclerc was fighting an all-out war on Santo Domingo. At first, things seemed to go well for the French. The Spanish section of the island was quickly occupied, with the help of the local white population. Some black garrisons surrendered to advancing French brigades. In ten days Leclerc had captured all of the key coastal ports and forts and was preparing an offensive into the interior. But Toussaint L'Ouverture remained beyond his grasp, and another black general, Jean Jacques Dessalines, rampaged through the countryside, slaughtering every white person he found—and any black or mulatto who tried to help them.

An attempt at negotiations failed and on February 18, 1802, Leclerc launched an offensive against L'Ouverture's interior stronghold, Gonaives. After some hard fighting and heavy losses on both sides, several black generals switched their allegiance and supported Leclerc. The

French commander added to the threat of his oncoming bayonets lavish promises of money and power to those who joined him in a pacified Santo Domingo.

On February 23, L'Ouverture ambushed a French force of five thousand men a few miles from Gonaives. For a while the French teetered on the brink of a rout. But their commander, General Donatien de Rochambeau (son of the general who was George Washington's partner at Yorktown) rescued the situation with a moment of bravado. Tossing his hat into the ranks of the oncoming blacks, he shouted: "My comrades, you will not leave your general's hat behind!" The French infantry wheeled and soon had L'Ouverture's men on the run. The next day the French stormed Gonaives and burned it.

Leclerc was losing men—as many as two thousand in a single battle. Also, for the first time he noticed a strange illness creeping through his army. Soldiers weakened without warning; in a day they were too sick to walk. Then came black vomit, yellowing skin, convulsions, and death. Neither Leclerc nor anyone else realized that this "yellow fever" was produced by a tiny female mosquito now known to scientists as *Aedes aegypti*.

Breeding in pools of stagnant water in cities, towns, and army camps, *Aedes* triggered devastating epidemics in the Caribbean, South America, and tropical Africa, with death rates as high as 85 percent. But the French commander pressed his offensive. He was as determined and ruthless as his imperious brother-in-law. Soon other black generals— notably Henri Christophe—switched sides.

On May 1 Toussaint L'Ouverture agreed to peace

terms: He would give up power and retire with a respectable bodyguard to a plantation in the interior. His generals and officers would receive equivalent ranks in the French army, which soon became 50 percent black.

Why did Toussaint surrender? Probably because he learned that Napoleon had signed a definitive treaty of peace with the British at Amiens. This left Toussaint and his soldiers at the mercy of Bonaparte's vastly superior numbers and weaponry. The black leader capitulated, hoping to get the best possible deal from Leclerc. L'Ouverture's murderous second in command, Dessalines, sullenly accepted similar terms on May 6, 1802.

For a few weeks an uneasy truce prevailed on Santo Domingo. It did not last because *Aedes aegypti* was hard at work, decimating the French regiments. Noting Leclerc's growing weakness, a watchful L'Ouverture began intriguing for a comeback. But Leclerc was watching him, too. Lured to a nearby plantation without his usual armed escort, the black leader was seized, thrown on a ship, and deported to France as a common criminal. There, Napoleon deposited him in a damp, freezing dungeon in a fortress in the Jura Mountains on the Swiss frontier, where L'Ouverture died a year later.

President Jefferson was stunned by Toussaint's surrender and abrupt removal. Not quite able to believe the news, he wondered if it were the other way around—that Leclerc had surrendered. The White House would have welcomed that news. It was vivid evidence of how much the president's attitude had changed since he made his fulsome promise to Pichon the previous July.

Jefferson's change also reflected a new development on the diplomatic front. On May 6, 1802, Tobias Lear had made an unexpected appearance in Secretary of State Madison's office. General Leclerc had expelled him from Santo Domingo for protesting the imprisonment of two U.S. ship captains who had aroused Leclerc's ire. One of them had been accused of slandering the French army in American newspapers because of his report of the sanguinary seizure of Cap Francois.

More shocking was what Lear had learned from talking to officers in Leclerc's army: In France, republicanism was "exploded." France needed a king now, and the man the soldiers were backing was, to no one's surprise, Napoleon Bonaparte. President Jefferson's long love affair with the French Revolution was coming to an ironic close.

4

Frustration All Around

In France, Minister Plenipotentiary Robert R. Livingston demanded an interview with Foreign Minister Talleyrand. The New York aristocrat bluntly asked if Spain had retroceded Louisiana to France. Talleyrand looked him in the eye and with practiced chicanery denied that any such transaction had occurred. Undaunted, Livingston proceeded to put pressure on the foreign minister as if the answer had been affirmative.

There were still some $5 million in unsettled U.S. claims against France that were outside the boundaries of the Quasi-War damages renounced in the Treaty of Mortefontaine. Livingston used the claims as a weapon in this opening clash with Talleyrand. The minister suggested that the French give West Florida and New Orleans to the United States, and the U.S. government would undertake to settle the claims out of its own affluent pockets.

"None but spendthrifts satisfy their debts by selling their lands," Talleyrand curtly replied. He paused and added something significant. "But it is not ours to give."

The foreign minister was admitting that, thus far, the French had not persuaded the Spanish to cede either West or East Florida. There was a powerful faction at the Spanish court that opposed giving Louisiana or the Floridas to Napoleon. It was led by former foreign minister Manuel de Godoy, once the lover of Queen Dona Maria Luisa. Thus far in 1802, pliable King Carlos IV had yet to sign the legal documents transferring the huge western territory to France. Napoleon, growing impatient, told his ambassador to warn the queen and Godoy that "if this system [of delay] is continued . . . it will terminate in a thunderbolt."

Nevertheless, Livingston had no difficulty confirming the eventual transfer of Louisiana. It was the talk of the Paris salons. Several publishers had brought out books extolling this new western empire. "Louisiana is a very favorite measure here," Livingston told Madison.

Irritated and frequently frustrated, Livingston nonetheless retained his fondness for France and the French people. At times his letters were a veritable rhapsody of praise for their joie de vivre, their good manners, and the beauty of their women. The French were the happiest people he had ever encountered, he said, because they made women the "rosy links" in their society.

But when Livingston attended an official dinner at which everyone, male and female, was bedecked in gorgeous finery worthy of a royal court, he experienced the odd sensation of being out of place because he was too republican for Napoleonic France. Livingston told Secretary of State Madison that he was playing down his "democracy" and was careful not to criticize any aspect of this new authoritarian state, in which people from all walks of life had the opportunity to seek their fortunes—as long as they were willing to surrender the right to speak their minds.

This balancing act was a tribute to Livingston's diplomatic talents. But behind the scenes he did not hesitate to continue to oppose the French acquisition of Louisiana. When Talleyrand rebuffed his offer to buy West Florida, Livingston returned with an even more ambitious proposal. Would France agree to sell to the United States all of Louisiana north of the Arkansas River? That would permit France to retain New Orleans and the ports on the Gulf of Mexico to check British power in the Caribbean. Meanwhile, the Americans would become a buffer between these French possessions and the British in Canada.

When Talleyrand rejected this proposal, Livingston approached the British ambassador to France, Lord Whitworth, and tried to get him excited about the threat posed by a Napoleonic army in the Mississippi Valley. If they were suddenly yearning for the lost province of Louisiana, wasn't it logical to assume a similar desire would be directed at Canada? Livingston also went to work on the Spanish ambassador, muttering dark warnings in his ear about the likelihood of a French descent on Mexico. Finally, Livingston wrote to Rufus King in London and urged him to stir up British opposition to the retrocession.

All these seemingly good ideas came to naught. The British were so desperate for peace that they professed a near indifference to Napoleon's colonial ambitions. The new prime minister, Henry Addington, was reducing the royal army to forty thousand men, beaching much of the royal navy, and junking the income tax that had funded Britain's war machine. When Rufus King queried the new foreign secretary, Lord Hawkesbury, about the French acquiring Louisiana, he received a perfunctory "highly interesting."

This indifference was truly dismaying news. There was apparently no hope of playing off one superpower against the other. The United States was on its own against the French juggernaut.

In Washington, D.C., an increasingly anxious Jefferson decided to put new pressure on the French with a letter to Livingston. It was sent via a special envoy, Pierre Samuel Du Pont de Nemours, who had emigrated to the United States in 1799 and begun a number of businesses that would make his name famous in the coming decades. Du Pont was returning to France to raise capital for his companies, and said he was more than willing to approach Napoleon on the United States' behalf.

Jefferson's letter gave Du Pont severe doubts about being the president's messenger. Jefferson had left it unsealed, giving the Frenchman carte blanche to read it. The message opened with the literary equivalent of an artillery barrage:

The cession of Louisiana and the Floridas by Spain to France . . . completely reverses all the political relations of the U.S. and will form a new epoch in our political course . . . There is on the globe one single spot, the possessor of which is our natural and habitual enemy. It is New Orleans, through which the produce of three-eighths of our territory must pass to market, and from its fertility it will ere long yield more than half our whole produce and more than half our inhabitants. . . . The day that France takes possession of N Orleans . . . seals the union of the two nations who in conjunction can maintain exclusive possession of the ocean. From that moment, we must marry ourselves to the British fleet and nation.

Jefferson explained to Livingston his opening paragraphs were not intended as a "menace" but as a frank statement of the political situation in America. "Every eye in the United States is now fixed on this affair of Louisiana. Perhaps nothing since the revolutionary war has produced more uneasy sensations through the body of the nation."

Jefferson went on to reiterate his desire for peace and understanding with France. He noted the "strong sympathies" for the French republic that still existed in the minds of many Americans. There was only one way for France to retain this sympathy: sell the Floridas and the city of New Orleans to the United States.

In a separate letter to Du Pont, Jefferson took an even tougher line. He told the Frenchman that the sale of the Floridas and New Orleans would only be a "palliation." The president insisted that France's occupation of Louisiana would be an enormous mistake. It would eventually trigger a war between France and the United States that the British would enter as a U.S. ally. This was not a development

Jefferson welcomed. He reminded Du Pont of how long and fervently he had professed his friendship for France. He was being open with Du Pont because he hoped that the impromptu envoy would be able to impress the French government more effectively than Livingston, whom Talleyrand was treating as a person of no consequence.

A final metaphor communicated how deeply the situation was agitating the president. Louisiana might seem no more than "a mere make weight, a speck" in the settlement of peace terms between England and France. But it was "the embryo of a tornado which will burst on the countries on both sides of the Atlantic and involve in its effect their highest destinies." The letter to Livingston was so important that the president begged Du Pont to make sure that Madame Du Pont would deliver it "with her own hands" if anything happened to him during the Atlantic voyage.

Du Pont totally disagreed with the tone and implications of Jefferson's letter. For one thing, he was certain it would offend Napoleon, whose patronage he had hoped to obtain on his visit. One did not make threats to the conqueror of Europe: "To say, 'Give us this land or else we will take it' is not at all convincing." Napoleon, and every other Frenchman, would instinctively say: "We will defend it."

As for marrying the United States to the British fleet and nation, Du Pont was even more appalled. That would be leading the United States into "a trap." He insisted that the British "detest and always will detest" the United States because they were rivals for commercial supremacy on the ocean. An alliance would inevitably lead to "persecutions" that would drive the United States back into the arms of France after wasting millions of dollars and thousands of lives in a pointless war.

Moreover, the Peace of Amiens made it clear that the British were sick of war and not inclined to marry their diminished fleet to anyone. Napoleon would only conclude from Jefferson's letter that the American president was bluffing—and that he was not very good at this brand of international diplomacy. There is little doubt that Du Pont was correct on all points.

His French patriotism aroused, Du Pont advised Jefferson that if he hoped to negotiate with France, he had better start by declaring the United States had no interest in the west bank of the Mississippi. He added a sermon on the aggressive tendencies of the United States. There was no question in Du Pont's mind that a great many western Americans were eager to conquer Mexico.

After discussing a number of alternatives, Du Pont suggested a strikingly original solution to the oncoming confrontation with France: buy Louisiana and the Floridas. There was no point in appealing to past friendship and the importance of the world's only republics remaining at peace with each other. The sole answer to an amicable solution was money.

Du Pont urged Jefferson to calculate how much a war would cost—the expense of building warships, organizing an army, paying sailors and soldiers—and offer France a reasonable sum for Louisiana and the Floridas. No matter how high the price might climb in the bargaining, it would still be cheaper than a war, and the conquest would be "poisoned neither by hatred nor by human blood."

Du Pont's reply forced Jefferson to do some hasty backtracking. In another letter, he denied he was threatening France. "It is as if I saw a storm tomorrow and advised my friend not to embark on the ocean today," he claimed. Clinging to his metaphor, he argued that foreseeing the storm did not make him "the cause of it." Nor was his warning a threat because the storm was not "produced by my will." Totally capitulating to Du Pont's injured French patriotism, the president confessed he was all too aware of the danger of an alliance with Great Britain. "It would only be better than to have no friend," he wrote.

By this time, there was not much left of the letter to Livingston. Confusing matters still more, the president dashed off a letter to the minister that would go through the regular mail, in which he wrote that the letter Du Pont would deliver was not to be construed as a sign that he was ready to go to war. He also admitted that he might have ventured into the province of the secretary of state— evidence that Jefferson knew how badly he needed the cool intellect of James Madison to navigate these shoal waters.

Aside from temperament, is there an explanation for Jefferson's erratic behavior? A probable answer is the ferocious attacks on his policies and reputation by aggressive Federalist editors who were hoping to undo the Republicans' narrow victory in 1800. This was a new experience for this thin-skinned man and his party. When the Federalists were in power, it was the Republican newspapers that had been on the attack, and Jefferson had covertly participated in not a few of their assaults.

In the spring of 1802, one of the Republican editors who had led the press campaign against the Federalists turned on the president and began giving him a very unpleasant taste of this partisan medicine. Scottish-born James Callender thought Jefferson should reward him for his previous services by making him postmaster of Richmond. When the president demurred, Callender began publishing in the *Richmond Recorder* Jefferson's indiscreet letters of earlier years, in which he praised Callender for his smears of Presidents Adams and Washington and enclosed substantial checks to keep the calumnies coming.

Also very much in the fray was the *New York Evening Post,* a newspaper founded by Alexander Hamilton. The *Post* tirelessly warned readers that Jefferson's drastic reductions of the navy and army, inspired by the "inviolable and universal peace" promised in the Treaty of Mortefontaine, were endangering the nation's safety. In the Federalist bastion of Massachusetts, the *New England Palladium* spewed even nastier venom on "the democratic emperor" and his supposed Republican simplicity, which was supported by a hundred toiling slaves at Monticello. As Louisiana became a topic of concern throughout the country, the Federalists roasted Jefferson and his party for their past pro-French sympathies and wondered sarcastically how they would deal with these new neighbors, who preferred to settle most disputes with the bayonet.

On May 1, 1802, Secretary of State James Madison sent a letter to Robert Livingston that was drenched in gloom. Louisiana "becomes daily more and more a source of painful apprehensions." Livingston's latest letters had made it clear that "no hope remains" that France might abandon the project. Madison could only urge Livingston to return to the attack, reminding Talleyrand that the "worst events are to be apprehended" if France went ahead. Livingston should also renew his effort to buy the Floridas and New Orleans. While the secretary of state declined to name a price, the United States would consider the purchase "a most precious acquisition" and "great liberality" would be displayed to consummate the sale.

The melancholy tone made it clear that Madison did not have much hope that anything would come of this diplomacy. With Santo Domingo all but conquered, there seemed to be little that the United States could do to prevent Napoleon Bonaparte from building Talleyrand's wall of brass in the great valley of the Mississippi River.

5

Aedes Aegypti
to the Rescue

On Santo Domingo, yellow fever continued to decimate General Leclerc's army. He managed to conceal its impact and maintain an appearance of strength. But he depended more and more heavily on the support of the black generals who had switched to his side, especially Henri Christophe and Jean Dessalines.

On June 11, 1802, Leclerc wrote to Napoleon: "If the First Consul wishes to have an army in Santo Domingo in the month of October, he must have it sent from France." By that month, the harried general estimated his twenty-thousand-man force would have dwindled to four thousand demoralized troops. "The ravages of sickness here are too great for words. Not a day passes without my being told of the death of someone whom I have cause to regret bitterly."

Leclerc said his own health was declining rapidly. "Man cannot work here much without risking his life . . . the government must seriously think of sending me a successor. It is quite impossible for me to remain more than six months." By that time, he hoped to be able to hand over the colony in a state of peace. But he gloomily added that his health was "so wretched" he wondered if he could last that long.

Into this delicate situation exploded stunning news from France. Napoleon Bonaparte had decided to reinstitute slavery on Guadaloupe and, when the time seemed right, on Santo Domingo. In the meantime, the slave trade was again authorized on both islands. Worst of all was a clause in the law that henceforth barred "men of color" or mulattoes from calling themselves citizens of France. This privilege had played a vital role in keeping the island's tens of thousands of mulattoes on the side of the whites.

Bonaparte had yielded to pressure from refugee planters from Santo Domingo and from numerous merchants in Le Havre and other French ports who had grown rich on the slave trade. His wife, Josephine, who was born in Martinique and whose family had owned a sugar plantation on Santo Domingo, was also rumored to have played a part in the decision to restore slavery.

Toussaint L'Ouverture had persuaded many former slaves to return to the sugarcane fields to work as draftees in the service of the state. They had done so reluctantly, and had not reacted well to his seizure and deportation. When the news of their possible reenslavement reached them, they rose in fury at this betrayal of the revolution's promise of liberty. French soldiers and civilians were attacked everywhere on the island.

General Leclerc was amazed by the ferocity of the blacks' assaults. "They die with incredible fanaticism—they laugh at death; it is the same with the women," he reported. The astonished French commander concluded he would have to kill everyone above the age of twelve, a policy he proceeded to put into brutal practice. But it did not prevent whole regions of Santo Domingo from remaining in violent insurrection.

By August 6, a demoralized Leclerc virtually accused Napoleon of being the source of his woes. "I entreated you, Citizen Consul, to do nothing which would make them anxious about their liberty until I was ready," he wrote. "That moment was rapidly approaching." But the law authorizing the slave trade and reestablishing slavery in Guadaloupe destroyed the "moral force" Leclerc had tried to establish as a spokesman of the French Revolution's ideals. Now, he could "do nothing by persuasion. I can depend only on force and I have no troops."

Bluntly, the distraught general told his brother-in-law that he would have to send a new army and "above all money." That potent word sent bitterness swelling through Leclerc's soul. He inveighed against "being left without funds as I have in a country where purchases are made only for their weight in gold." With money he also might have "got rid of much discontent" by bribing some black leaders.

If the first consul had been a witness to the difficulties he had overcome and the results he had obtained, Leclerc wrote, Bonaparte too would be grieved "to see all that I have done here on the point of being destroyed." Still, Leclerc had hopes of succeeding by brute force. "I make terrible examples, and since terror is the only resource left to me, I employ it." In the town of Tortuga, he hanged sixty out of four hundred fifty rebels. Now everything there was in "perfect order."

But the situation was worsened by merchants and former plantation owners who were arriving daily from France, thinking the island was pacified. They spoke of nothing but buying slaves, further enraging the blacks. It almost seemed as if there was "a general conspiracy to prevent the restoration of San[to] Domingo to the Republic."

Leclerc's own health continued to decline. Although he vowed to serve Napoleon "with the same zeal" he had displayed in other campaigns, he was now so weak that he was no longer able to ride a horse. "You must send me a successor," he warned the first consul. With 60 percent of his officers dead, Leclerc saw no one on the island who could replace him. If Napoleon continued to "abandon us to ourselves," Santo Domingo would be lost and "once lost you will never regain it."

Further worsening Leclerc's situation was the revised policy that Secretary of State James Madison had instituted toward Santo Domingo's civil war. The U.S. government made no attempt to stop American merchants from trading with the black rebels, shipping them guns and ammunition as well as food. The enraged French threatened to send captured blacks to the United States, where they would spread slave revolts throughout the South.

"The infernal French at this moment are vomiting all their wretched blacks upon our coast," reported one Southerner's letter reprinted in a Washington paper. The story turned out to be a Federalist fiction aimed at influencing the 1802 congressional elections.

In June 1802, relations between France and the United States were aggravated by an extremely hostile article published in the *Gazette de France,* a newspaper that was regarded as the French government's mouthpiece. The article descanted on how the French army in Santo Domingo had found in U.S. ships well-oiled guns and ammunition destined for the black rebels. What was behind this betrayal of Jefferson's promise to help France regain the colony? Unquestionably it was the United States' ambition "to rule over the new world and to place under its yoke all the West-India colonies."

There was only one way to prevent this obnoxious newcomer from achieving such power, the *Gazette* article continued: "France's acquisition of Louisiana would create an impenetrable barrier to America expansion" and be a "counterpoise to the domination of the United States." Talleyrand's wall of brass was still alive and well in the French vision of a regained colonial empire.

The article created a sensation when it reached the United States. Federalist newspapers called Jefferson's administration weak and naive. They were doing nothing about this looming threat of a hostile Napoleonic France. It made the Jeffersonians' policy of reducing the country's army and navy look more idiotic with every passing day. The situation was not improved by statements supposedly made by angry French officers on Santo Domingo that when the French army got to Louisiana, it would "bring the United States to its senses."

Secretary of State Madison called in Chargé d'Affaires Pichon for some very tough talk. The *Gazette de France* article seemed to imply that France was planning to try to split up the United States. Madison told him the scheme would not work. The Westerners and the Easterners shared a common language and the same political ideals. Even if the strategy succeeded, the secretary added, the Atlantic states would remain strong and such meddling would make them France's inveterate enemy.

President Jefferson followed up this lecture with an equally blunt conversation. He warned Pichon that for ten years France had been pursuing an anti-American foreign policy. If they kept it up now, with a friend of France in the White House, the policy would inevitably end up making an alliance with Great Britain "universally popular" in the country.

Poor Pichon was already a very unhappy man. General Leclerc had not only blamed him for his failure to obtain money and supplies from the United States. He had also wrathfully accused him of being more devoted to the U.S. government than to France. Infuriated by Pichon's advice to tread lightly with the Americans, Leclerc had called him a *miserable*, a *fripon* who was probably making money on the side from the trifling amount of supplies he had managed to buy.

Although Pichon saw his diplomatic career collapsing before his eyes, he stubbornly sent his government the advice he thought it needed. He tore into the article in the *Gazette de France,* which was almost certainly sponsored by Talleyrand. France was pursuing a ruinous policy toward the United States. Instead of preferring a strong and independent ally to help them oppose the power of England, they were talking about "repressing their growth by force."

This policy, he concluded, would throw the Americans "inevitably under the hand of England." Pichon urged Talleyrand, and by implication Napoleon, to pay more attention to the reports he kept sending them of the United States' amazing growth. It was far wiser "to be resigned to their future power" and thus "acquire the merit" of approving what "the force of events will give them in spite of us."

In Europe, meanwhile, the ingenious Minister Plenipotentiary Livingston had developed another angle of attack. When rumors swirled through Paris of how badly things were going in the conquest of Santo Domingo, the New York grandee wrote an unctuously sympathetic letter to Talleyrand, expressing his concern that General Leclerc's wife, Napoleon's beautiful sister, Pauline, was being exposed to the unhealthy climate of the island during the hot season.

Livingston wondered if Madame Leclerc would be interested in retreating to New York City for a few months. His brother, Edward Livingston, was the mayor, and the ambassador assured Talleyrand that Edward would be happy to lend Madame Leclerc his town house, which was "in the best and the healthiest situation in that city." On the other hand, if she preferred a country residence, Pauline would be more than welcome in his own Dutchess County mansion, Clermont, on the majestic Hudson River.

Livingston never received a reply to this artful invitation. Pauline remained in Santo Domingo. Livingston later said that he hoped the suggestion would stir gratitude in the first consul's heart, if Talleyrand passed it on. It was also a sly way of telling the foreign minister that Livingston knew the creation of Talleyrand's wall of brass was not going as smoothly as Bonaparte had predicted.

Undeterred by the foreign minister's snub, Livingston went to work on a far more ambitious communication, nothing less than a state paper analyzing the futility of France's acquisition of Louisiana. This "memorial" was an argument aimed not at Bonaparte but at the men around him, and at other thoughtful Frenchmen whose opinions might influence the government's policy.

An overseas colony, Livingston argued, was only valuable if a country had surplus population to send to it or surplus capital to invest in it. France had neither. A chronic shortage of capital was crippling that country's attempt to become a manufacturing nation in competition with England. Worse, overseas colonies had to be guarded "at great expense in men and money" from hostile powers.

Moreover, ten years of warfare had so badly damaged France's West Indies possessions, in particular Santo Domingo, that millions would have to be invested in slaves, buildings, and agricultural equipment to make them productive again. Livingston boldly predicted that "ages will elapse before Santo Domingo will cease to drain the wealth & strength of France without an equivalent return." Other overseas colonies in South America (French Guyana) and in the East Indies also needed capital investment to make them profitable.

All this information led to the pertinent question: What

use was Louisiana to France? Livingston's answer was: worse than nothing. Developing the vast territory would require a staggering investment in slaves to clear the land. That meant a far slower return on the invested capital once the land began to produce. Then there was the question of what would be grown: Many of its commodities, such as sugar, were already being produced in huge quantities in the West Indies. As for lumber—the northern American states exchanged it with the French West Indies for molasses, which the Americans turned into rum. Since the island colonies did not make rum, the molasses was otherwise useless, so for all practical purposes, the lumber was acquired free of charge. Lumber from Louisiana would destroy this thriving trade.

What about populating Louisiana with French emigrants? That, too, would require a huge initial investment. It would be ten or even twenty years before those people would begin to create a profitable economy. Would they be a market for French exports? Not likely. French wine would not survive long in a hot climate. And shipping French goods up the Mississippi to western Americans was a very expensive way to transport anything. The cost could not compete with goods pouring into the West from British and U.S. merchants in Philadelphia and New York, who had a burgeoning network of canals linking local rivers that enabled them to sell on "cheap & easy terms."

Livingston next turned to the danger of a collision between France and the United States on the Mississippi. The mere threat of such an event was likely to create an atmosphere of hostility toward France, sharply reducing

U.S. enthusiasm for its products. Livingston saw only one solution to the problem: France should sell the port of New Orleans to the United States at once, reserving for herself the perpetual right of entry. No American would object to this provision. The sale would be an act of generosity and wisdom that would guarantee the warmest possible friendship between the United States and France. In years to come, perhaps a colonized Louisiana would become a place where French manufacturers would be able to sell their goods to their U.S. friends.

The American minister had his memorial translated into French and ordered twenty copies from a printer, distributing them to influential Frenchmen in Napoleon Bonaparte's entourage. It was a neat way for Livingston to give the back of his hand to Talleyrand and his stonewalling tactics. The memorial was an artful document. The first half, the devastating critique of the value of Louisiana to France, was nicely masked by the second part, the pie-in-the-sky vision of Louisiana's prosperity if Napoleon decided to sell New Orleans to keep the Americans happy.

There was only one thing wrong with this well-thought-out essay: it was unlikely to have any impact on Napoleon Bonaparte, a man who did not think in terms that had meaning to ordinary people. Profit and loss were far less important than an extension of his imperious will which had become synonymous in his mind—and in the minds of millions of his followers—with French power in all parts of the world.

This reality became ominously clear to Livingston and many other people in August 1802, when a blatantly engineered plebiscite made Bonaparte first consul for life. A majority of the French people voted against the idea. But Napoleon's younger brother, Lucien Bonaparte, the minister of the interior, threw out the no votes and announced that the Man of Destiny had won, 3,600,000 to 8,374. Anyone who objected was swiftly taken into custody by Joseph Fouche, the ruthless minister of police.

A discouraged Livingston wrote to Secretary of State Madison in September: "There never was a government in which less could be done by negotiation than here—There is no people, no legislature, no councilors—One man is everything."

6

The Dying General

On Santo Domingo, the military situation continued to deteriorate. In mid-September, General Leclerc wrote a despairing letter to Napoleon. For the past four months he had survived in his "horrible situation" by "adroitness." He had no army worth mentioning. Yellow fever was killing 100 to 120 men a day and "a great part" of the black troops he had seduced from their allegiance to Toussaint had deserted him. The rebels had seized control of the mountainous part of the island, and the general's only hope of ousting them was "a war of extermination which will cost me many men."

After reiterating his need for reinforcements and money, Leclerc again urged Bonaparte to select his successor. He added that he was "thinking seriously of quitting this colony" without waiting to hear from the first consul. No ordinary general would display such effrontery to his commander in chief. Leclerc was taking advantage of his status as Napoleon's brother-in-law.

"I leave this [letter] to go back to my bed, where I am

hoping not to stay long," Leclerc concluded, underscoring his weakened health. This optimism about an early recovery soon proved to be unjustified. On November 2, 1802, the dashing General Leclerc died on Santo Domingo.

This bad news only made First Consul Bonaparte more grimly determined to take Santo Domingo and Louisiana as well, according to his original plan. He shipped more troops to the embattled island and made General Donatien de Rochambeau their commander. He ordered a separate twenty-thousand-man expedition to Louisiana to prepare to sail under the command of another highly regarded general, Claude Perrin Victor.

An unexpected problem delayed Victor's expedition. The Spanish king was still stalling on putting his signature on the documents that officially transferred Louisiana to France. Greed was the chief reason for the delay. The king's son-in-law wanted to enlarge the kingdom of Etruria to make him look convincingly royal. When the ruler of the adjoining duchy of Parma conveniently died, Napoleon ordered French troops to "liberate" Parma and add it to the new kingdom. That produced a signature— but the king and his councilors, including the powerful Manuel de Godoy, stubbornly declined to include a cession of the Floridas in the agreement. Godoy had acquired a profound loathing for Bonaparte, which led him to risk a military thunderbolt to frustrate the Corsican's plans. Nevertheless, Napoleon told General Victor to sail for New Orleans as soon as he had provisioned his ships and properly equipped his men.

A dismayed Robert Livingston, who had exerted himself

to find out as much as possible about the French negotiations with Spain, reported to Secretary of State Madison that France had "cut the knot." Spain had ceded Louisiana. Livingston included in his letter a report from a U.S. merchant whom he had persuaded to visit General Victor at Helvoet Sluys, the port in Holland where his ships were being fitted out. Introducing himself as a man from Louisiana, the American found Victor remarkably talkative.

When the merchant asked the general what he intended to do about the U.S. right to deposit goods in New Orleans for export in accordance with their 1795 treaty with Spain, the general called the treaty "waste paper." Pierre Clement de Laussat, who was to accompany Victor as prefect of the province, claimed he had never even heard of the treaty. This supposed ignorance strongly suggested that the French planned to inflict a lucrative export duty on every pound the Americans shipped from New Orleans.

The general told his American visitor that he had 2.5 million francs from the French treasury to finance the expedition—a relatively trifling sum. Victor expected the people of Louisiana to pay most of his expenses. Livingston warned Madison that Victor's expenses would be heavy. "The number of officers, civil and military, with their suits [suites] is great," and they were empowered to "draw" on the local populace. The U.S. minister concluded that the first act of this new government would be "the oppression of their people and our commerce."

Worse, Livingston added, was evidence that there would be "an early attempt to corrupt our people." Here Livingston was worrying about General Victor using some of his 2.5 million francs to bribe western Americans to secede from the United States and become a French protectorate. There was also a strong probability of a French attack on Natchez, the southernmost U.S. port on the Mississippi, "which they consider a rival of New Orleans." The collisions feared by Secretary of State Madison were already part of the French agenda.

Before mailing this potentially explosive letter, Livingston decided to call on Talleyrand and find out if General Victor's aggressive plans had his approval. Talleyrand unctuously assured the minister that the first consul had given him "the most positive assurances" that U.S. rights in New Orleans under their treaty with Spain would be "strictly observed." Livingston asked him why the officers in command of the Victor expedition did not know this rather salient fact. Talleyrand smoothly assured Livingston that Victor and his lieutenants would be given copies of the Spanish treaties before they sailed and ordered to "conform strictly to them."

Livingston thought Talleyrand's promises were worthless. He told Madison "it would be well to be on our guard and above all, to reinforce the Natchez." If Victor were confronted with a strong and resolute U.S. Army, he might well have second thoughts about throwing his weight around.

General Victor's secret orders from the minister of the navy, Admiral Denis Decres, and from Talleyrand make it clear that Livingston's distrust was well founded. Decres, writing in Napoleon's name, told Victor to avoid a war with the United States. But he was also ordered to "maintain sources of intelligence," especially in Kentucky. This was a coded directive to bribe Americans to spy and agitate in France's favor. Even more important was the need to "fortify" himself against the Americans by forming alliances with the Indian nations east of the Mississippi.

To this plan of studied deception and betrayal Talleyrand added his own predictably duplicitous advice. Every time the Americans raised "pretensions" about their rights in New Orleans, Victor was to tell them that he had written to Paris for instructions and was expecting an early reply. Meanwhile, he was to stand his ground and soak the Americans for all they were worth.

By the time Livingston's warning letter reached Washington, President Jefferson and Secretary of State Madison were absorbed by a far more immediate worry than General Victor's expedition. Late in October they learned that Don Juan Ventura Morales, the Spanish intendant (the ruler of New Orleans and Louisiana) had closed the port to U.S. goods and products. Morales claimed that he did so under a clause in the 1795 treaty with Spain, which stipulated that Americans enjoyed the right of deposit as neutrals in England's war with France and Spain. The Treaty of Amiens had ended the war and with it the United States' neutral status.

No one believed this specious argument. Virtually every American saw the closure as part of France's plans for Louisiana. The French, they assumed, wanted to abolish the right of deposit in order to inflict maximum export duties on U.S. goods when they took possession. General Victor's unvarnished comments about his plans lend credence to this assumption. Added weight would seem to come from the timing of the order to take this explosive step: Carlos IV sent the command to the intendant the day after the king had finally signed the documents transferring Louisiana to France.

Some historians, influenced by other documents in the Spanish archives, claim the Spanish had local motives. The order was supposedly aimed at punishing the Americans, who were abusing the right of deposit by smuggling gold and silver through New Orleans. Another possible motive cited by other historians was the desire of the circle around Manuel de Godoy to embarrass Napoleon. They argue that the French were as surprised as everyone else by the Spanish move, which they supposedly heard about in a dispatch from Chargé d'Affaires Pichon.

The doubletalk from Talleyrand that Livingston was encountering in France suggests that the French may have pretended to be surprised. The advantages they would gain from abolishing the right of deposit—and the size of General Victor's army—suggest that the Americans of 1802 were probably correct about the real reason for the intendant's order. While Godoy and his circle had a degree of influence on King Carlos IV, the French presence in the Spanish court was also pervasive. A bribed or intimidated Spaniard could easily have persuaded the witless king to ease France's path to power in New Orleans with the order to the intendant.

Bolstering this conclusion is Talleyrand's reaction when he supposedly heard the news of the suspended rights for the first time. He wrote a letter to the Spanish ambassador to France, offering congratulations from the first consul, who was "pleased with the firmness [Spain] has shown in this circumstance." All but salivating over the coming wall of brass, the foreign minister added: "The difficulty of maintaining it [the suspension] will be less for us than would have been our establishing it."

The Spanish decree swept through all parts of the United States with tornado force. William Hulings, the American vice consul in New Orleans, voiced the initial concern in an October 1802 letter to Madison: "The season for the cotton from the Natchez and other produce from the settlements higher up [the Mississippi] approaches. The difficulties and risks that will fall on the citizens of the United States, if deprived of their deposit, are incalculable."

Hulings reminded Madison that the right of depositing the westerners' products in warehouses ashore was absolutely vital because their flatboats were "so frail, and so subject to being sunk by storms." They could not be converted into "floating stores, to wait the arrival of sea vessels to carry away their cargo."

From Natchez to Kentucky and the booming Ohio and Indiana territories rose a roar of rage that all but rattled windows in Washington, D.C. Phineas Bond, an English consul, told his government, "Scarcely anything has happened since the Revolution . . . which has so much agitated the minds of all descriptions of people in the U.S. as this decree."

The governor of Kentucky warned President Jefferson that the citizens of his state were "very much alarmed."

If the Spanish policy were not altered immediately, it would "at one blow, cut up their present and future prosperity by the roots." The governor of the Mississippi Territory said that the cancellation had "inflicted a severe wound on the agricultural and commercial interest of this country." State and territorial legislatures in the West passed thunderous resolutions denouncing the move.

An agitated Secretary of State Madison fired off a letter to South Carolinian Charles Pinckney, the U.S. minister to Spain, ordering him to make the strongest possible protest of "this direct and palpable violation" of the treaty of 1795. Pinckney was to inform the Spanish government that the president of the United States expected them not to "lose a moment" in countermanding the intendant's order, which Mr. Jefferson hoped was the product of personal caprice.

Madison was sure that Pinckney understood "the sensibility of our western citizens" to the Spanish order. Their feelings were more than justified by what was at stake. "The Mississippi is to them everything. It is the Hudson, the Delaware, the Potomac, and all the navigable rivers of the Atlantic states, formed into one stream." In 1801, Kentucky and the Mississippi Territory alone exported produce worth $1,622,672 through New Orleans. In 1802 the volume would rise by at least 50 percent. Already Kentucky had more than a half-million dollars' worth of grain and cotton on the river, heading for the Mississippi's only ocean port.

Madison's letter would take at least six weeks to reach Madrid. Meanwhile, President Jefferson had to deal with "the shout for war" that was echoing through all parts of the country. The Charleston *Courier* declared that "we would be justified to ourselves and to the world" if the United States took possession of New Orleans by force of arms, and reclaimed "the advantages of which we have now been unjustly deprived." Other newspapers, many of them edited by Federalists, made similar declarations.

Among the loudest shouters for hostilities was Alexander Hamilton in the *New York Evening Post*. In private letters General Hamilton mocked Jefferson's dilemma. Having abolished internal taxes and reduced the armed forces to a shadow, the president was now faced with a major war, without the men or the money to fight it. Hamilton said similar things in his newspaper.

Seldom has a U.S. president confronted a more threatening situation. For Jefferson, the timing could not have been worse for another reason. On September 1, 1802, his former friend and partner in slandering the Federalists, James Thomson Callendar, had published in the *Richmond Recorder* the worst imaginable accusation for a southern-born president. Callender reported it was widely known in Virginia that the widowed Jefferson had fathered four or five children by an attractive mulatto slave, Sally Hemings.

Soon Federalist newspapers throughout the country were printing a mocking song "supposed to have been written by the Sage of Monticello":

Of all the damsels on the green
On mountain or in valley

A lass so luscious neer was seen
As the Monticellian Sally.

The accusation, still debated by contemporary historians, seemed to open floodgates of newspaper abuse of Jefferson's reputation. Soon another story circulated about his attempted seduction of the wife of his best friend, John Walker. Then came editorial recollections of Jefferson's poor performance as governor of Virginia during the revolution, when he revealed a singular ineptitude at rallying the state to repel the invasion of a few thousand British soldiers in 1780–1781.

When Congress met in December to receive the president's annual message, Jefferson astonished everyone by barely mentioning the turmoil in the West. He spent most of his time praising himself and his party for the prosperity and tranquility of the country. Federal revenues from import duties had totaled $12,280,000, which enabled the administration to pay down $5 million of the national debt. Only in his closing lines did Jefferson remark that French possession of Louisiana would produce "a change in the aspect of our foreign relations." He did not say a word about the looming crisis created by the cancellation of the right of deposit at New Orleans.

This Jeffersonian attempt to stick his and the nation's head in the political sand did not work. General Alexander Hamilton called the message "a lullaby." He reminded readers of the *Evening Post* that he had "always held that the unity of our empire, and the best interests of our nation require that we annex all the territory east of the

Mississippi, New Orleans included." Hamilton was talking about Spanish East and West Florida, which could only be seized by an act of war.

Other Federalist newspapers assailed Jefferson's timidity and indecisiveness. Reflecting this viewpoint, the House of Representatives called on the president to give them all the pertinent papers on the Mississippi crisis.

As this debate began, a letter to Secretary of State Madison from William C. C. Claiborne, governor of the Mississippi Territory, revealed both the Western inclination for war and the paucity of their resources to wage it. Claiborne said he had "about two thousand militia, pretty well organized." With six hundred of these men, he thought it would be easy to seize New Orleans, "provided there should only be Spanish troops to defend the place."

Two thousand militiamen would do very little harm to General Victor's twenty thousand veteran troops. The nervous proviso that the militiamen were only eager to fight Spaniards is another indication of how close Napoleon Bonaparte was to seizing control of Louisiana at gunpoint. If General Victor's expedition reached New Orleans on schedule, the Man of Destiny might soon disturb Jeffersonian America's tranquility and wreck its prosperity.

7

A War Hero to
the Rescue

Thomas Jefferson was still determined to stifle a rush to war over the Mississippi crisis. The president had talked with the Spanish ambassador to the United States, the Marquis de Casa Yrujo, who was married to the daughter of the Republican governor of Pennsylvania. Yrujo, out of touch with the inner politics of the Spanish court, had assured the president that Intendant Morales had revoked the right of deposit on his own say-so. Letters from New Orleans, quoting the Spanish governor of Louisiana and the secretary of the province as being opposed to the revocation, further encouraged Jefferson to accept this dangerously wrong idea and take a peaceful line. He was relying on Madison's letter to Pinckney to extract a turnaround in Madrid.

In the House of Representatives, the Jeffersonian majority moved to shut down the debate as quickly as possible. In response to the Federalist call for papers on the

Mississippi crisis, a Republican congressman proposed a resolution that blamed the breach of contract on "the unauthorized conduct of certain individuals rather than want of good faith" on the part of the king of Spain.

The Republicans asserted that Congress would rely "with perfect confidence on the vigilance and wisdom" of the president. Mr. Jefferson would, they were sure, uphold the rights of the United States and gain satisfaction for any "injuries" inflicted by the revocation.

The Federalist minority objected to the claim that the House had perfect confidence in the vigilance and wisdom of Thomas Jefferson. Their amendment striking out the phrase was voted down, two to one, and the Republican resolution passed by an equally overwhelming vote. When the Federalists again tried to call for papers, this time on the cession of Louisiana to France, the House majority leader, John Randolph, mockingly asked why they wanted to deal with the executive branch of the government after announcing they had no confidence in it.

In the Senate, the Federalists were not so easily silenced. More and more they saw the Mississippi crisis as their last hope of overturning Jefferson's ascendancy. Almost to a man, Federalist senators demanded war to redeem the national honor. Their speeches and editorials in Federalist newspapers resounded through the West, where a warlike mood increased with every passing day of apparent inaction by the president. Thousands of people signed memorials and remonstrances demanding an immediate solution to the crisis.

Early in 1803, Jefferson and Madison decided that they

had to do something more visible than write letters to the king of Spain and assure everyone that the revocation of the right of deposit was a personal quirk of Intendant Morales. On January 11, Jefferson nominated James Monroe as envoy extraordinary to the French government. He was to join Robert Livingston in persuading Bonaparte to sell New Orleans and the Floridas. Simultaneously, Madison asked the House of Representatives to allocate $2 million to facilitate the negotiations.

The secretary of state composed a statement for the House committee that emphasized the administration's peaceful policy. He said the money would help America avoid war, "the great scourge of mankind." Republican majorities in both branches instantly approved these measures.

Underscoring the urgency of the situation was the peculiar fact that Jefferson made the nomination without even asking Monroe if he was willing to go. On January 13, 1803, the president wrote Monroe a revealing letter. After describing the war fever in the West and the problem of pursuing peaceful solutions that were "invisible," Jefferson informed Monroe that he was the only man who could rescue the situation.

"You possess the unlimited confidence of the administration and of the western people; generally of the Republicans everywhere; and were you to refuse to go, no other man could be found who does this," he wrote. Moreover, Monroe's appointment had "already silenced the Feds here" in Washington.

His emotion mounting with every line, Jefferson

continued: "All eyes, all hopes, are now fixed on you; and were you to decline, the chagrin would be universal, and would shake under your feet the high ground on which you stand with the public." Although it was hardly needed, the president added an ultimate summons: on the outcome of Monroe's mission "depends the future destinies of this republic."

Fifteen years younger than the president, Monroe had been a devoted follower since Jefferson had recruited the earnest, humorless ex-soldier as an aide during his turbulent Revolutionary War governorship and later offered to tutor him when he decided to study law. Monroe had bought land in Albermarle County and seldom made a political or personal move without consulting Jefferson. In the footsteps of his mentor, he had completed a term as governor of Virginia. Previously, Monroe had been a courageous officer in the Revolutionary army (he had been wounded leading a charge in the battle of Trenton) and represented Virginia in the U.S. Senate.

Public service paid poorly and Monroe had an expensive and beautiful New York–born wife. Jefferson knew Monroe was planning to retire from politics and devote his energy to developing his large landholdings in Kentucky. The president admitted he was asking Monroe to make a "great sacrifice" to abandon this plan, in which he had already invested much time and money. All Jefferson could offer him was the consoling thought that "some men are born for the public." They were destined to serve the human race "on a broad scale."

Who could refuse such a presidential summons? Monroe

accepted the appointment. The Federalist reaction was anything but friendly. While Monroe undoubtedly had strong support in the West, thanks to his Kentucky landholdings and the large number of Virginians who had migrated over the mountains, he also carried with him a taint that made him something of a gamble for Jefferson.

In 1794, President George Washington had appointed Senator James Monroe the U.S. minister to France. Monroe replaced Federalist Gouverneur Morris of New York, who had become more and more alienated by the French Revolution's slide into mob terror. At the same time, Washington dispatched another envoy, John Jay, to England to try to resolve looming problems with that nation about several matters, especially their treatment of U.S. ships and seamen.

Washington assumed Monroe would do his best to strike a neutral but not unfriendly stance in Paris. Instead, Monroe was about as neutral as the *Gazette de France*. In his first appearance, a welcome before the chamber of deputies, the new minister hailed the "fortitude, magnanimity and heroic valor" of the French soldiers and sailors in their struggle against England and her "impious coalition of tyrants." An appalled Washington ordered his secretary of state, Edmund Randolph, to reprimand Monroe for "the extreme glow" of his address.

The reprimand did no good. Monroe careened through his next two years in France, making blunder after blunder. He seldom if ever took the U.S. side in any dispute. His dispatches regularly hailed French military successes as if they were fighting America's battles. At one point he even urged Washington to join the war, arguing that U.S. men and ships would cause England's swift collapse. When Washington spurned the idea, Monroe suggested that he loan France $5 million dollars, which the envoy was sure American voters would be happy to finance with a special tax.

For Washington, the last straw was the discovery that Monroe had secretly offered to send a series of pro-French letters to the violently Republican Philadelphia newspaper, the *Aurora*. The letters would be described as informal reports from a gentleman in Paris to a friend in the city of brotherly love. Washington and his cabinet grimly concluded it was time to recall Monroe. The attorney general of the United States declared that the Virginian was "furthering the views of a faction in America, more than the peace and happiness of the United States." Monroe returned to America in disgrace, and many people thought his political career was ruined.

Jefferson made sure Monroe survived. Monroe's fervent support of France was nothing less than an expression of Jefferson's own intense feelings. The man from Monticello was a prominent guest at a public dinner that hailed Monroe as a hero when he arrived back in the United States. Jefferson helped him write a vigorous defense of his conduct in Paris and backed him for the governorship of Virginia. He heaped praise on Monroe as a man of surpassing integrity. "Turn his soul inside out, and you would be unable to find a spot," he declared. But Monroe remained an extremely partisan star in the political firmament.

The Federalists made this all too clear by ferociously

attacking Monroe's appointment. One angry Federalist senator saw it as a slur on President George Washington's memory. "The measures of Washington are to be reviled, his admirers wounded," he stormed. The nominee's shaky status among his own party soon became apparent. Some moderate Republicans considered Monroe an extremist whose avowed friendship with the radical French revolutionaries of 1794 might offend Napoleon Bonaparte. The special envoy won the Senate's approval by a mere three votes—15–12.

Five days later, on January 18, Jefferson asked Congress to approve and finance another mission. It would be led by his private secretary, Captain Meriwether Lewis, and Lieutenant William Clark. Their orders were to explore the "Missouri country"—the northern half of Louisiana, watered by the Missouri River—and report on the Indians, the soil, and the geography of that part of the continent. Was it suitable for white settlement? Was there a route from the headwaters of the Missouri to the Pacific Ocean?

Jefferson had been thinking about this expedition for a long time. Not without some arm-twisting, he had obtained permission to launch it from the Spanish government, insisting that its purpose was scientific and peaceful. In his confidential message to Congress, he admitted that it might also provide "an extension of territory" for the United States's rapidly increasing population.

Even more important was the need to know more about the region if the United States had to defend it against a British lunge from Canada. Secretary of the Treasury Gallatin saw this as a distinct possibility if a new war broke out between France and England. Jefferson wanted to know how many Spanish troops were in the area and where forts might be built to resist a British attack.

The Mississippi crisis gave the Lewis and Clark expedition a new urgency. Now the attack might come from a French army. Jefferson had no difficulty in extracting approval and an appropriation for the expedition from Congress. It was now much closer to a military reconnaissance than a scientific exploration, but Jefferson saw no need to tell that to anyone but a handful of insiders.

On February 16, 1803, a month after Monroe was confirmed, Federalist Senator John Ross of Pennsylvania rose to assail the envoy and the Jefferson administration. Ross lived in Pittsburgh, which qualified him to be a spokesman for Westerners as well as for the moneyed men of the East. Word of his forthcoming philippic had swirled through Washington, and a crowd of excitement seekers packed the Senate chamber for the show.

Ross began by blaming the Mississippi crisis not on the intendant but on the Spanish government in Madrid, calling it nothing less than a studied affront to the U.S. government and its people. If such an insult were inflicted on the citizens of an Atlantic coastal port, imagine the uproar that would ensue. But Jefferson and his government of Easterners had no sympathy for Westerners. They were telling them that their crops must rot on their lands while the government sent an envoy across the Atlantic to negotiate with France.

"Why submit to a tardy uncertain negotiation?" Ross demanded. "Why not seize New Orleans and Florida now and negotiate later?" The Westerners were ready to fight, but President Jefferson was attempting to "put to sleep" this spirit of resistance. Was he going to wait until the French were in possession, and the city and surrounding territory were "armed and garrisoned?" By that time, the men of the West would have lost confidence in their government.

As for the prospect of France selling New Orleans and the Floridas, Rose said there was only one way that would happen. He had seen it stated in U.S. newspapers that the $2 million voted by the House of Representatives would be used to bribe "certain influential persons" in Bonaparte's government.

Senator Robert Wright of Maryland leaped to his feet screaming "Order!" He accused Ross of betraying confidential information that had been given to the Senate in secret session. Wright's real purpose was to derail Ross's attempt to remind everyone that the Federalists had fought the Quasi-War rather than pay bribes to Talleyrand and his corrupt associates.

Ross appealed to Vice President Aaron Burr, the Senate's presiding officer, to rule on Wright's accusation. Burr said he found it hard to see what was confidential about a newspaper rumor of incipient bribery. Senator Wilson Cary Nicholas, the Republican majority leader, gave Burr a frosty glare and demanded that the galleries be cleared and the chamber's doors closed to the public.

A reluctant Burr issued the order and an infuriated Ross refused to say another word. "I will never speak upon this subject with closed doors!" he cried.

This blatant attempt to stifle debate did not go down

well with the Senate or the public. Two days later, after the upper house had approved the $2 million subsidy to Monroe's mission, the solons voted to open their doors and Ross resumed his speech.

Recapitulating his call for immediate action, Ross asked if any nation would respect a government that remained passive under such humiliating treatment as the Spaniards had inflicted on the Americans at New Orleans. What was Jefferson's remedy? It was "a secret . . . only committed to confidential men behind closed doors." With brutal sarcasm, Ross called the president's solution a "sovereign balm" that would supposedly heal America's "wounded honor." Could anyone believe this glorified "patent medicine" would extinguish "the devouring spirit [of the French revolution] which has desolated . . . Europe?"

Ross submitted a series of resolutions, affirming the U.S. right to the free navigation of the Mississippi and a right of deposit at New Orleans, and authorizing the president to call out fifty thousand militia from the states of the West and South to take immediate possession of the city. Another resolution called for an appropriation of $5 million to finance this act of war.

Federalist newspapers and spokesmen hailed Ross's speech as a masterpiece. Alexander Hamilton said it could not fail to "excite the applause of every American." The *Evening Post* published the text of the speech a few days later and called the resolutions "the Federalist Plan." A war, Hamilton admitted, was undoubtedly a calamity. "But national degradation is greater and besides, it is always inevitably followed by war itself."

A few days later, Senator Samuel White of Delaware seconded Ross with a speech that focused on the risk Jefferson was taking with his policy of delay and negotiation. He wondered what Americans would do when the "sluggish Spaniard" was replaced by the "vigilant and alert French grenadier." Instead of a garrison that would surrender at the Americans' mere approach, "we shall see unfurled the standards that have waved triumphant in Italy, surrounded by impregnable ramparts, and defended by . . . disciplined veterans."

White piously declared that he attributed "the best motives" to President Jefferson and Secretary of State Madison. He was sure they did not want to embroil the country in a war. He "deprecated its horrors as much as any man." But he was also sure that "the business can never be adjusted abroad." The only question the United States could decide was whether "it shall be a bloodless war of a few months, or the carnage of years."

The next day, Senator Gouverneur Morris of New York followed White with a slashing speech that drew on Morris's wide knowledge of Europe to ridicule Jefferson's preference for negotiation. He dismissed the president's reliance on Ambassador Yrujo's claim that the revocation of U.S. rights in New Orleans was a quirk of Intendant Morales. Republican newspapers had published a letter from Yrujo, asserting this as fact and insisting on his country's friendly feelings for the United States. Morris said: "I cannot commit the interests of my country to the goodness of his [Yrujo's] heart."

Morris drew a dark portrait of Napoleon as a conqueror

who could not rest on his laurels. His power depended on new conquests. He reminded his listeners of how often the French revolutionists had expressed their hunger to regain Louisiana. Now they had a general and an army with the power to satisfy this hunger. Did President Jefferson think he could extract Louisiana from Bonaparte by singing him a lullaby? "Is he a child whom you may win by a rattle to comply with your wishes?"asked Morris.

Speaking directly to Jefferson and his followers, Morris mocked the possibility of using persuasion on Bonaparte. "He wants power; you have no power. He wants dominion; you have no dominion . . . that you can grant. He wants influence in Europe, and have you any influence in Europe? What in the name of heaven are the means by which you would render this negotiation successful?"

The country had only one choice, Morris concluded: war. He reminded his listeners of the conduct of America in "her infant years," when the threat of an invading British army was brandished to subdue the rising fervor of the revolution. "Did we then hesitate? Did we then wait for a foreign alliance?" No. Instead, Americans "threw our oaths of allegiance in the face of our Sovereign, and committed our fortunes and our fate to the God of battles." This was the conduct of Americans when they had not yet become an independent republic. Now that they had gained that "elevated station," were they about to desert it?

Delivered with surpassing eloquence before galleries crowded with admiring listeners, Morris's speech infuriated the Republicans. One of their best orators, Senator Stevens

T. Mason of Virginia, took the floor. By then it was 7:30 and candles illuminated the Senate chamber. Saying he was "indisposed," Mason asked the Senate to adjourn until tomorrow, which would permit him to make an extensive reply to Morris.

It was common knowledge that Mason was seriously ill, but the Federalists brusquely objected to adjournment. They wanted to maneuver Mason into making a weak speech, leaving Morris triumphant. A vote was called for and on a show of hands, Vice President Burr announced a tie, 12–12. He thereupon voted against adjournment, making clearer than ever his alienation from Jefferson's administration.

An angry Republican senator called for a "division"—a procedure in which the clerk of the Senate recorded each vote. This time the tally was 13–12 in favor of adjournment. A furious Morris discovered that Federalist Senator William Plumer of New Hampshire had voted with the Republicans. Plumer said he was merely being considerate to the obviously ill Senator Mason. "No man in public life," Morris snarled, should let "personal convictions" interfere with loyalty to his party.

There was no longer any doubt that the Federalists were betting the future of their party on the hope that Monroe's mission would fail and that President Jefferson would stand revealed as the same weak-kneed character who had behaved so badly when he was governor of revolutionary Virginia in 1780. The Jeffersonian Republicans remained grimly committed to following the president down the perilous path he had chosen. First Senator Mason, and then Senator James Breckinridge of Kentucky assailed the arguments of Senators Ross, White and Morris.

The Republicans sarcastically asked why the Federalists were so eager to go to war over the supposed insult of the suspended right of deposit at New Orleans. Why was it that they never called for war when the British navy inflicted far more brutal humiliations on U.S. ships and seamen in the 1790s? Captains had been flogged before their crews and U.S. citizens kidnapped into servitude on British men-of-war. How did President Washington and the Federalists respond? They negotiated with England. Why was President Jefferson a coward for trying to negotiate with France?

Breckinridge, who had emerged as the West's leading spokesman, closed his speech by admitting that if the negotiations failed, war would be the only alternative. He offered a set of resolutions, which he urged the Senate to adopt in place of Senator Ross's proposals. These resolutions revealed how much the Federalist attack had thrown the Republicans on the defensive. Breckinridge called on Congress to authorize state governors to organize and equip eighty thousand militia who should be ready to march "at a moment's warning." A corps of volunteers was also authorized to serve for a specified number of years to provide a standing army that would be more reliable than the militia, whose terms of service were seldom longer than a few months. Money would also be appropriated to finance this formidable host and to erect arsenals on the western waters to supply them with guns and ammunition.

The Republican majority obediently adopted Senator

Breckinridge's program. But there was an unconvincing, déjà-vu quality to their resolutions. Among the politicians of the West, as well as their less warlike compatriots in the East, Senator Ross and his fellow Federalists were still the ones who had displayed the courage to defy Napoleon Bonaparte from the start of the Mississippi crisis. If Monroe's mission failed, there was little doubt that the Federalists would fill the country with gloating I-told-you-so's and insist that George Washington's favorite soldier, General Alexander Hamilton, be named to command the U.S. Army in its march on New Orleans. A president who had announced in his inaugural address that there was no real difference between Republicans and Federalists might find it difficult to resist this demand.

8

Between Peace and War

While the congressmen and senators orated, President Jefferson and Secretary of State Madison pushed ahead with their plan to negotiate before declaring war. Monroe came to the White House for long conversations with his two fellow Virginians. They told him that his mission was to purchase New Orleans and West and East Florida from France. They assumed Napoleon had obtained these latter possessions from Spain. Monroe was authorized to pay as much as fifty million francs, or $9,375,000. If the French refused to sell, he was to negotiate a treaty confirming the U.S. right to deposit goods in New Orleans as well as at the mouths of other rivers emptying into the Gulf of Mexico.

The envoy was pleased with his assignment. He wrote to his friend George Clinton, the governor of New York, that he was undertaking the mission "with pleasure" because it gave him an opportunity to pursue a goal he had "always had much at heart." He meant Franco-American friendship, which had eluded his naive professions of amity during his previous sojourn in Paris.

Monroe may have been enthusiastic, but he was also broke. Jefferson found himself wishing he had not talked so much about the frugality of his administration. Under the Federalists, envoys had sailed to their overseas destinations aboard U.S. Navy frigates. Robert R. Livingston had been allowed this privilege, but he was a National Republican. Such public transportation was out of the question for Old Republican Monroe.

"Mr. Madison's friendship, and mine for you, being so well known," Jefferson wrote, "the public will have an eagle eye to watch if we grant you any indulgence out of the general rule."

By "public" the president meant the opposition party. Sharpening their eagle eye was the denial of a frigate to Federalist Rufus King, who had recently requested to be relieved from his post in London. This meant Monroe would have to pay for a cabin aboard a merchant ship for himself, his wife, and his two daughters.

To finance this accommodation and the other expenses of the trip, Monroe sold Secretary of State Madison more than two hundred pieces of solid silver flatware as well as three dozen pieces of Sevres porcelain plates and a white-and-gold china tea set. He had bought this splendid tableware in Paris, and had paid $4,000 to have it crated and shipped to the United States. It was an ironic glimpse of how far from simplicity this staunch Old Republican had drifted under the influence of his well-born wife. The less-than-simple lifestyle of his friend Mr. Jefferson at Monticello may also have been influential.

On the eve of Monroe's departure from Washington,

the Republicans underscored their all-out support of his mission by giving him a dinner at M'Laughlin's Tavern in the nearby village of Georgetown. Every Republican congressman and senator in Washington attended this affair, along with Chargé d'Affaires Pichon, Ambassador Yrujo, and other members of the diplomatic corps. Numerous toasts were drunk. Yrujo proposed: "May the powers of Europe never be divided from the United States but by the ocean." Monroe's toast was much more concerned with domestic political worries: "To the Union of the states— may political discussion only tend to cement them."

New York's chief Jeffersonian newspaper, *The American Citizen,* noted that one prominent Republican had not been invited to the dinner: Vice President Aaron Burr. "This is not the effect of negligence," wrote the *Citizen's* editor, James Cheetham, "but of mature deliberation. It is a just and awful sentence pronounced upon his past misconduct and was designed to be so understood."

Monroe and his family set out for New York, where he hoped to find a ship departing for France. By then it was February; wretched weather and even more wretched roads turned the journey into an ordeal that left Monroe so exhausted that a doctor ordered him to bed. Rest restored him and he soon found a cabin available on the ship *Richmond.*

While awaiting final instructions from Secretary of State Madison, Monroe wrote a letter to Jefferson that revealed how much was at stake in his mission. He admitted that "the resolutions of Mr. Ross" had produced "a great effect on the publick mind . . . and more especially in the western country." He also recognized the "unanimity" among the American people regarding the right to free navigation of the Mississippi "and its importance to every part of the U. States."

From the intensity of the public's feelings on this issue, Monroe concluded that if the negotiation ended in some sort of compromise that would leave control of the Mississippi in the hands of "a foreign power," the result would be intense disappointment and disapproval, especially in the West. Nothing less than "complete security for the future" was going to satisfy the American people.

"The consequences of a disappointment are not easily calculated," Monroe noted nervously. "If it restored the federal party to power and involved us in a war, the result might be fatal." The envoy did not elaborate on the nature of this fatality—the independence of the United States, or the future of the Republican Party. One suspects the latter because in the next few sentences, he suggested to Jefferson that the retention of the loyalty of the Westerners was so important, a threat of war should be the "ultimatum" of his negotiations. A war under Republican auspices would be better than under a "monarchial" administration.

Monroe's resort to ideological extremism with the use of that undemocratic slur, the favorite slander flung at the Federalist Party by the Jeffersonians, was another indication of his anxiety. It was not easy for this fervent Francophile to contemplate threatening France with war. He had to justify it in his own mind by picturing the Federalists as evil allies of England.

Still determined to give Monroe's assignment all the

fanfare in their power, the Jeffersonians saluted the envoy's departure aboard the *Richmond* on March 9, 1803, with blasts from the federal artillery in the fort at the tip of Manhattan Island and another cannonade from the fort on Governor's Island in New York Harbor. The editor of the *American Citizen* declared he entertained "not the least doubt of his mission." Monroe's letter reveals that the envoy himself did not share this partisan braggadocio.

As Monroe and his family endured the wintry Atlantic, the Federalist press attacked his mission with rumor and invective. Boston's *Columbian Centinel* reported that Monroe had been told to purchase New Orleans and the Floridas, even if the asking price was $40 million. Reminding its readers that Monroe would be dealing with the infamous Talleyrand, the paper speculated that with *beaucoup d'argent* "even Mr. Monroe may be able to effect purchases where Citizen Talleyrand has a commanding influence."

The *Centinel's* editors called the $2 million voted by the House "secret service money" and asked its readers: "What will Bonaparte think of us? He will consider us blockheads to be gulled, and he will shrug his shoulders at Mr. Monroe and say 'Gad you have come in a lucky time—we want funds. I did not expect your millions but since you have brought them I will gladly accept them as a pledge of the attachment between the two countries. Pay it to my faithful Talleyrand and tender to Mr. Jefferson the homage of my dearest love.'"

In New York, writing under the pen name Pericles, General Alexander Hamilton had already denounced Monroe's mission as folly. It was "in every respect the weakest measure that ever disgraced the administration of any country." There was, the general declared, "not the remotest chance that the ambitious and aggrandizing views of Bonaparte will commute the territory for money." The Ross resolutions, aka the "Federalist Plan," was the only solution to the crisis: Seize New Orleans and the Floridas and negotiate later.

From Europe came a letter from Pierre Du Pont de Nemours, who had reached Paris and delivered Jefferson's belligerent letter to Robert Livingston. Still anxious to keep France and the United States at peace, Du Pont urged Jefferson to avoid a clash with Spain or France over the closure of New Orleans. The unofficial envoy said that he had talked with Talleyrand and other officials and thought they would be willing to sell the Floridas for $6 million. In return, he urged Jefferson to accept French rule of everything west of the Mississippi. He even enclosed a draft of a treaty that he thought the French would accept, confirming this dangerous arrangement.

Du Pont was a dolorous example of the trouble with using special envoys. He thought he was an insider, but he did not even know France had failed to obtain the Floridas. Talleyrand was obviously using him to lull the Americans into going along with the main point of French policy, the occupation of Louisiana. Jefferson and Madison believed that Du Pont knew what he was talking about, and in their final instructions to Monroe they reiterated orders to bid for the Floridas.

Although the administration still talked and sought peace, privately the president prepared for war. Jefferson wrote urgent letters to the governors of the western states and territories, urging them to press Indian tribes on the east bank of the Mississippi to sell their lands to the United States. The Indians would almost certainly be prime targets of French money and influence. The Spaniards already maintained a network of support with annual "presents" to powerful tribes, such as the Creeks and Choctaws.

Jefferson's letter to William Henry Harrison, the territorial governor of Indiana, did not mince words about his intentions. While he insisted that U.S. policy aimed at living in peace with the Indians, he also declared: "Should any tribe be foolhardy enough to take up the hatchet" their "whole country" would be seized and they would be driven across the Mississippi. The government's ultimate goal was a "final consolidation" of U.S. power on the east bank of the Mississippi by persuading the local Indians either to become peaceful farmers or seek new lands west of the river.

Jefferson wanted this consolidation to stretch from the mouth of the Mississippi to "its northern regions." He was anxious to be prepared "against the occupation of Louisiana by a powerful and enterprising people." It was vital to present a "strong front" on the western border and enable the Americans along the Mississippi to defend themselves. The president went down a veritable laundry list of small tribes, such as the Cahokias, the Piorias, the Kaskaskias, and urged Governor Harrison to buy their lands by offering them enough money to let every individual in the tribe live in ease for the rest of his or her life. It would be "a small price" for the government and worth every cent.

"The crisis is pressing," Jefferson wrote. "Whatever can

now be obtained must be obtained quickly. The occupation of New Orleans, hourly expected, by the French, is already felt like a light breeze by the Indians." Under the hope of French protection, Jefferson feared the Indians would "immediately stiffen against cessions of lands to us." He wanted Harrison to get to work on doing "at once what can now be done."

Jefferson stressed to Harrison that his letter was "private and friendly." He wanted it "sacredly kept in your own breast." The reason is obvious. Written on February 27, 1803, nine days before Monroe sailed, the letter revealed a president who was deeply worried about the prospect of the French in Louisiana. This was not the confident, soothing stance that Jefferson was presenting to the public. The letter also revealed a defensive psychology that was the total opposite of the aggressive, preemptive-strike policy of the Federalists.

Would Jefferson's plan have worked? There was a slightly frantic, last-minute quality to his preparations for the arrival of Napoleon's legions. While urging haste, the president simultaneously admitted that the Indians were already reacting against the Americans at the mere "breeze" of the rumored French arrival. If one adds Monroe's anxiety, it seems more than a little dubious that these ex-lovers of France would have been able to wage war against the aggressive generals and public officials of Napoleon Bonaparte.

Also evident at this point in the crisis was Jefferson's assumption that no matter what Monroe achieved in his negotiation about U.S. rights on the Mississippi, there would still be a large French army in Louisiana to worry about. No one, including the president and his astute secretary of state, imagined that Bonaparte would abandon such an immense swath of the continent once he occupied it.

In Washington, Secretary of State Madison worked on pliable Chargé d'Affaires Pichon, who somehow wanted to extricate peace from the coming collision of France and the United States on the Mississippi. The president participated in this exercise. In some ways it resembled the "good-cop-bad-cop" routines of modern police procedure, but there is no evidence of a preconceived collusion.

On January 12, 1803, Jefferson invited Pichon to dinner at the White House and assured him that Monroe's appointment had "tranquillized" the angry Westerners. Pichon was quick to report this good news to Talleyrand. The president's friendship for France was apparently still a significant factor in the ongoing crisis.

Two days later, Madison summoned Pichon to his office and told him in the grimmest tones that France's plans were propelling both countries into a disastrous war. In no-nonsense phrases, the secretary of state warned the French diplomat that the Americans insisted on obtaining New Orleans and the Floridas. This would enable them to separate themselves from their foreign neighbors by natural boundaries. More and more Americans were growing cotton on the upper waters of West Florida streams that emptied into the Gulf of Mexico. The free navigation of these rivers was inseparable "from the very existence of the United States," Madison said.

The Secretary of State assured Pichon that the United

States did not want its citizens to emigrate beyond the Mississippi. A colony west of the river would "infallibly" become a separate state. This would almost certainly lead to a "collision with the East" that would have disastrous consequences for the American people. Only one thing could lead to such an unfortunate emigration—a war between France and the United States, which would provoke a U.S. invasion of Louisiana. The president was sending Monroe to France to avert this calamity. A "prompt conclusion" of Monroe's mission would also avert "political combinations"—an alliance with England—that the United States also sincerely wished to avoid.

Pichon rushed a dispatch to Paris with this unnerving threat. The West might be temporarily tranquilized, but the Americans were unmistakably threatening war if Monroe's mission failed. "The crisis grows greater every day," Pichon warned, "and we cannot push it into the distant future." Pichon added that he would "fail in my duty" if he did not tell Talleyrand that "these feelings of concern which Mr. Madison expressed" were "generally felt" by the American public.

Not long afterward, Pichon supplemented this warning with another note: "Necessity is forcing Mr. Jefferson to give up his pretensions and scruples against an English alliance. I have observed at table [in the White House] that he redoubles his kindnesses and attentions to the British chargé d'affaires."

While the Senate debated the Ross resolutions, Madison assured Pichon that there was no basis for the rumor that the governors of Pennsylvania, Kentucky, and Tennessee were gathering an unauthorized army at Pittsburgh to descend the Mississippi and resolve the crisis at gunpoint. (Just to make sure, he had written stiff letters to these three state executives, warning them not to launch such an adventure.) Talking to the French chargé at a public reception, the secretary of state added some dire remarks in tones loud enough for bystanders to hear every word. Madison said the nation was "in ferment," especially in the West. Only the people's confidence in the government prevented the Westerners from acting. The United States was extremely conscious that it held "the balance of power in the new world." It was time for European powers to realize this fact.

To reduce Western tensions, Madison persuaded Pichon to write a public letter to Intendant Morales in New Orleans, claiming that France disapproved of his decision to close the port. The secretary of state showed Pichon a letter from Robert Livingston in which he quoted Talleyrand's assurance to this effect. Madison remarked that if the foreign minister had put this statement in writing, a great deal of the uproar on the Mississippi would have been avoided. Now, at the very least, Pichon's public letter would help rescue France from the "odium thrown on her" as the suspected author of the policy.

The Jefferson administration was beginning to feel more and more like a man caught between the proverbial rock and a hard place. The president talked peace to the men of the West. His secretary of state talked war to the ruler of France. How long could this doubletalk continue without triggering an explosion?

9

All Eyes on Paris

In Paris, Robert R. Livingston continued his attempts to persuade Napoleon to abandon his dream of a colonial empire. The news of General Leclerc's death, which reached Paris early in the new year, had cast a pall on Bonaparte's vision of imperial glory. Livingston sensed that the Man of Destiny might be persuaded to change his mind about reestablishing New France in America.

Disgusted with Talleyrand's rebuffs and evasions, Livingston decided to pursue a new approach to the first consul, through his older brother, Joseph Bonaparte. Lazy and vain, Joseph liked to dabble in politics without committing too much thought or effort to a specific program or strategy. He had been the nominal head of the delegation that had negotiated an end to the Quasi-War with the Americans at his villa, Mortefontaine. He played a similar role in the negotiation of peace with the British at Amiens. At a diplomatic reception he startled Livingston by telling him that he would be glad to receive communications about Louisiana and pass them on to his brother.

Joseph told Livingston he had "access" to Napoleon "at all times." The first consul was "his own counsellor," the elder Bonaparte added, "[but] we are good brothers and he hears me with pleasure." In fact, this self-appraisal was on the modest side. Joseph had been the leader of the family during the years of Napoleon's ascendancy and still retained considerable influence with the first consul.

Livingston responded with alacrity to this invitation to backstairs intrigue, knowing that it might well involve *beaucoup d'argent*. The Bonapartes were at least as corrupt as Talleyrand. The minister first pumped Joseph for information about France's negotiations with Spain to obtain the Floridas. Reviving the proposal he had made to Talleyrand, Livingston suggested that many problems might be solved if Napoleon returned Louisiana to Spain and simply kept the Floridas and New Orleans, and then transferred them to the United States as a settlement for the millions of dollars in claims that U.S. merchants had against France.

Joseph Bonaparte's reply to this proposition was indirect but startling. He asked Livingston if the United States might prefer to buy Louisiana rather than the Floridas. Livingston strenuously denied any American interest in the larger territory. The United States had no desire "to extend our boundary" across the Mississippi. America only sought security, not "extension of territory." Still, the minister was more than pleased to learn that Spain was apparently still resisting the cession of the Floridas.

To demonstrate his friendship and admiration for the Bonapartes, Livingston now put forward a remarkable proposal: Why not persuade the first consul to give the

Floridas and New Orleans to his family as a refuge, should he be assassinated or killed in battle? France would be prey to "tyrants and popular demagogues" who would persecute the surviving Bonapartes. The territory would be placed under the jurisdiction of the United States. Furthermore, half the land would be sold to the Americans for a nice round sum, say 10 million francs—$2 million—and deposited in the Bonapartes' account to guarantee "the present splendor of your family."

Joseph's reaction to this vision of the Bonapartes in flight from their enemies was decidedly negative. But he agreed to present to his brother another part of Livingston's proposal, one that revived his early idea—selling the two-thirds of Louisiana that lay north of the mouth of the Arkansas River to the Americans. This would ensure that the British could not attack the province from Canada if a new war broke out between France and her chief rival.

When news of the suspension of the right of deposit at New Orleans reached Paris, Livingston went into diplomatic overdrive. He wrote a strenuous letter to Joseph Bonaparte, warning him that France and Spain were flirting with an American war and very possibly a U.S. alliance with England. The elder Bonaparte hastily backed away from this aggressive tone. He stiffly informed Livingston that henceforth he must address all his communications to Foreign Minister Talleyrand "who alone could inform you of the intentions of the government."

Livingston had by no means wasted his time with Joseph Bonaparte. He had penetrated Talleyrand's Paris version of a wall of brass and made the first consul aware of the urgency and anxiety that Americans felt about Louisiana. He had also planted the seed of another idea by telling Napoleon that the United States was not averse to acquiring a large chunk of the vast territory, which Livingston described as a "desert." He simultaneously communicated another favorite theme, that developing Louisiana would be "ruinously expensive" to France.

Along with outmaneuvering Talleyrand via Joseph Bonaparte, Livingston practiced another variety of the diplomatic art to disturb France's devious foreign minister. He never failed to pay elaborate attention to Lord Whitworth, the British ambassador, whenever they met at the weekly round of receptions and dinners. Whitworth was soon telling his foreign secretary in London that "the little intercourse which has arisen between him [Livingston] and myself gives a considerable degree of jealousy to Mr. Talleyrand."

Livingston also kept an eye on General Victor's army and fleet, which Napoleon had ordered to sail for Louisiana in October 1802. Admiral Denis Decres, minister of the navy, had been forced to divert ships, troops, and supplies to the embattled French army on Santo Domingo. This drain led to shortages that delayed Victor's expedition, until winter weather had produced an impasse that not even the Man of Destiny could surmount. Ice now blocked the port of Helvoet Sluys. Late in December, Livingston wrote to Secretary of State Madison: "The armament for Louisiana has not yet sailed; the civil officers are yet here [in Paris], if I am rightly informed by the minister [Talleyrand] from whom I had it yesterday."

In late January, Livingston passed on another important

piece of information: Napoleon had appointed General Jean Baptiste Jules Bernadotte, second only to the first consul in the hierarchy of the French army, to be ambassador to the United States. Livingston had immediately protested this shift of focus to Washington, D.C., especially when Talleyrand admitted that the general was not being given the power to negotiate a treaty. In his usual cavalier style, Talleyrand told Livingston he wanted information about the right of deposit in New Orleans—something he could just as easily have obtained from Charge' Pichon.

Livingston suspected another motive for the appointment of Bernodotte: the general would carry with him an aura of Napoleonic power and prestige that Talleyrand hoped would awe the Americans into accepting French occupation of Louisiana. The foreign minister also had the effrontery to tell Livingston that France was pleased to learn that Madrid had made it clear that the right of deposit at New Orleans was now something that Spain could grant or withhold, depending on what suited it best. France, he said, looked forward to doing the same thing.

Faced with such blatant stonewalling, Livingston struggled against bouts of depression. Diplomacy in Napoleon's Paris was a full-time job. If a minister hoped to be effective, he had to show up at every official and semiofficial reception in the crowded week. Livingston was proud that his wife had been invited to dine at Napoleon's table at the state dinners to which the diplomatic corps was invited twice a month. But these affairs were also an ordeal. They began with a parade at the Tuileries at noon, then a three-hour levee at which the first consul chatted with various diplomats; next came a dinner at 5:30, followed by a reception that lasted until the first consul deigned to depart, usually around eleven o'clock. "On such days," Livingston groused, "we may be literally on our feet for at least 9 hours, except for three quarters of an hour at dinner, for no meal is so short as a court dinner."

Toward the end of January, a discouraged Livingston wrote to Madison that he had talked to Bernadotte about U.S. merchants' claims against France and gotten nowhere. "Neither he nor anyone else can influence the councils of the first consul." Again underscoring his disgust with Napoleon's dictatorship, he advised Madison that "you can hardly conceive anything more timid than all about him are; they dare not be known to have a sentiment of their own, or to have expressed one to anybody." In such an atmosphere, Livingston began to wonder if there was any point in the United States keeping a minister in Paris, "where there is but one will and that will governed by no object but personal security and personal ambition."

There is little doubt that a year in Napoleon's Paris had extinguished any and all illusions about France in the mind and heart of this particular Jeffersonian Republican.

Nevertheless, Livingston stayed in the game. Adjusting his republican predilections to Napoleonic realities, on February 27, 1803, he wrote a fawning, almost cringing letter to the "Citizen First Consul" in which he apologized for intruding on the Man of Destiny's valuable time while humbly begging him to issue a statement declaring that U.S. rights at New Orleans would be upheld by France. He hoped Bonaparte would do this "as a profession of your good will." He also hoped that Napoleon would guarantee U.S. rights on nearby Florida rivers as further evidence of "your friendly disposition."

Even better would be a decision to sell the Floridas and New Orleans, of course. His government was ready to pay a generous price, which the money-short French treasury could undoubtedly use. If that idea failed to meet the great man's "approbation," perhaps a partial session or some sort of permanent commercial advantages could be worked out.

There was another worry that the minister hoped the first consul would permit him to mention: the possibility of an Indian uprising if France failed to continue the Spanish policy of purchasing the friendship of the "numerous and brave" tribes on the east side of the Mississippi. A massacre of the widely scattered white settlers would inevitably result. Livingston closed by begging Napoleon to forgive the length of his letter, which was due to his "extreme anxiety to remove all causes of dispute between France and the country I represent."

All Livingston got as a reward for his cringing was a ferocious rebuke from Talleyrand for daring to address the first consul directly rather than through him. The foreign minister was especially annoyed by Livingston's opening lines, which strongly implied that he was sure that Napoleon had not seen any of the numerous letters, memorials, and protests he had written in the previous twelve months. The rest of Talleyrand's letter was a sarcastic dismissal of Livingston's "solicitude" for France's finances, which were not in the least embarrassed, followed by the announcement that the first consul had now decided to send General

Bernadotte to Washington with the power to negotiate a new treaty dealing with U.S. rights on the Mississippi.

In his inimitably snide way Talleyrand was informing Livingston that he did not know what he was talking about and that he was wasting his time in Paris trying to reach an agreement about anything. Undeterred, Livingston fired back that the United States did not want a new treaty but a confirmation of the old one with Spain. "No change in the circumstances of the country [Louisiana] obliges them to relinquish [those rights] and they never will relinquish them but with their political existence."

In this atmosphere of thrust and parry around Napoleon Bonaparte's enormous power, Livingston learned of Monroe's appointment as an envoy extraordinary. Secretary of State Madison explained its necessity as a device to calm the passions of the Westerners, and he struggled to assure Livingston that the decision was not a reflection on his performance as minister plenipotentiary. But Livingston found it hard to see it from any other perspective. On March 3, 1803, he dutifully told Madison he would do "everything in my power to pave the way" for Monroe.

Livingston could not resist adding that Monroe's intrusion more or less cut the ground out from under his feet. "I had established a confidence that it will take Mr. Monroe some time to inspire," he wrote. To prove his case, he enclosed a copy of his letter to Napoleon, adding that he had written it "before I heard of Mr. Monroe's appointment." Livingston added that he had also established a certain "personal interest" that he would now have to relinquish. Here, the ambassador was probably referring to the *beaucoup d'argent* he had promised Joseph Bonaparte.

Livingston had good grounds for his doubts about Monroe's role in Paris. To put it in modern terms, the Virginian was the leader of the left wing of the Jeffersonian Republican party, a stance he had amply demonstrated in his previous ministerial stint. Someone with this ideological bent was not likely to be popular with Bonaparte, who was in the process of extinguishing the last flickering embers of French democracy. Glumly, Livingston wrote to Rufus King in London that Monroe "has greatly embarrassed my operations."

In another letter, the minister told Madison that a dispatch from Pichon, reporting Jefferson's remark that Monroe's appointment had "tranquillized everything," was just what the French wanted to hear. Livingston had been basing his diplomacy on warning Talleyrand that the West might explode at any moment and that an agreement was urgently necessary. The minister did not know about Pichon's follow-up dispatch after his talk with Madison in which the chargé had warned Talleyrand that the West still might explode. If Jefferson and Madison were playing a clever game with Pichon, it seems odd that they did not let Livingston in on the secret. More likely, Madison was still hard at work correcting Jefferson's tendency to put too much stress on the impressions of the moment.

Around Livingston swirled a world of power politics on which he kept a keen eye. Relations between England and France were by no means tranquil. Several important provisions of the Treaty of Amiens had not been fulfilled. France was supposed to evacuate the Netherlands, leaving it in a state of semineutrality. Bonaparte's army and navy were still operating in that hapless nation. Among other things, they were fitting out the Victor expedition, which looked suspiciously like an invasion fleet to the wary British.

The British were supposed to hand over to France the island of Malta in the Mediterranean. Their army and navy still occupied that strategic chunk of rock, which made it difficult if not impossible for Bonaparte to renew his interest in Egypt. There he and a French army had come to grief in a 1798 attempt to sever the British empire's lifeline to India.

Napoleon had not forgotten this humiliation. In August 1802 he had dispatched General Horace Sebastiani to the Levant and Egypt. From there he journeyed to Syria, plying local Moslem leaders with flattery and gifts. Meanwhile the British were in the process of withdrawing their army from Egypt, in accordance with the Treaty of Amiens. In February 1803, Sebastiani published in the semiofficial Paris *Moniteur* a highly provocative report on his journey, in which he estimated that Egypt could be conquered by as few as six thousand French troops.

Within a few weeks another French general, Charles-Matthieu Decaen, sailed for India with a large staff that could easily be used to raise and train native regiments. To England, such moves looked alarmingly like preparations for another Napoleonic attack on their eastern empire.

Even more upsetting to London was a French reoccupation of Switzerland after some local politicians revolted against the puppet government that Napoleon had installed there. Also dismaying was the way Talleyrand and Napoleon redrew the map of Germany, at the time a collection of small kingdoms, duchies, and principalities under the vague and mostly nonexistent government of the Holy Roman Empire. Taking advantage of Austria's helplessness, the French operated a kind of political tag sale during which German princes, including the king of Prussia, paid Talleyrand millions in bribes.

On February 20, the first consul sent a report to the French parliament that Robert Livingston read with all but obsessive attention. It discoursed with bombastic satisfaction on the health and wealth of France and its standing in the world. There was scarcely a part of the globe that was not discussed from the viewpoint of French power and influence. Bonaparte also had some hard things to say about the schemes of a "war party" in London. For Livingston the first consul's omissions were the most interesting part of his message. Bonaparte did not say a word about Spain, the United States, or Louisiana. This suggested uncertainty, indecision, and perhaps a drastic change of policy.

The tense atmosphere was soon compounded by the British equivalent of Napoleon's report to parliament. George III's speech from the throne on March 2, 1803, expressed his government's satisfaction with British prosperity and power in similarly self-satisfied tones. But the king's speechwriters expressed grave concern about French fleets and armies being fitted out in various ports, as if France were about to resume the war—and possibly invade England. Parliament responded by ordering the nation's militia to muster and prepare to bolster the reduced numbers of the regular army.

Behind the scenes, Britain had instructed Lord Whitworth to demand "a satisfactory explanation" for the conduct of the French government and its cavalier attitude toward maintaining peace. The British stand was bolstered by backing from Russia, which had no desire for a Napoleonic army in the Mideast. The young Czar Alexander urged the British not to surrender Malta. Whitworth was soon told to inform the first consul that London had decided to keep the island for another ten years as a countermeasure to France's refusal to evacuate the Netherlands and its seizure of Switzerland.

On March 12, 1803, Livingston trudged to yet another reception, this one in Madame Josephine Bonaparte's drawing room. The uncrowned queen of France presided over the entire first floor of the immense Tuileries Palace. While the ladies gathered in an adjoining room, Livingston stood wearily in the usual semicircle with his fellow diplomats, wearing his plain, black, republican suit. As usual, it contrasted starkly with the finery in which the others represented their royal masters. Napoleon entered with a gloomy expression on his face. He stalked around the semicircle, exchanging only a few terse words with several diplomats, including Livingston, passing the rest in surly silence.

The Man of Destiny halted in front of Lord Whitworth and glowered at him for a menacing moment. "I find, my lord, that your nation wants war again," Bonaparte snarled.

"No, sire, we are most desirous of peace," said the flabbergasted Whitworth.

"You have just finished a war of fifteen years!" Napoleon said. Apparently the first consul considered the five years in which England was at war with Royalist France during the

American Revolution part of the conflict that had erupted in 1793.

"It is true, sire, and that is fifteen years too long," Whitworth replied.

"But you want another war of fifteen years," Bonaparte insisted.

"Pardon me, sire, we are very desirous of peace," gasped Whitworth.

Growing angrier by the moment, Napoleon said heaven would take vengeance on the men who broke the peace of Amiens. France had no intention of invading England, he raged. There was not a single man of war in France's ports. All available ships had been sent to Santo Domingo. France sincerely wanted peace but Napoleon was thoroughly sick of British footdragging on the fulfillment of the treaty. "Malta must be evacuated or it is war!" Bonaparte said.

The prefect of the palace interrupted the irate first consul to whisper that Madame Bonaparte and many ladies were awaiting him in the next room. Napoleon strode away, leaving the appalled Whitworth fearing the worst. Spotting Livingston in the crowd, the British ambassador rushed over to him and repeated what Bonaparte had said.

Back in his residence, Livingston hurried to his writing desk and sent the news of Napoleon's explosion to Secretary of State Madison, remarking that renewed war might make Bonaparte more amenable to taking U.S. cash for the Floridas and New Orleans, if and when he pried them out of Spain's hands. At the very least he might restore U.S. rights in New Orleans and seek American aid to help him defend Louisiana. "I shall give all my attention to avail myself of circumstances as they arise, in which I hope shortly to receive the assistance of Mr. Monroe," Livingston wrote.

The American minister did not know that another force was being deployed to prevent the war that he feverishly hoped would force France to negotiate. After his ominous exchange with Bonaparte, Lord Whitworth fell back on a favorite British tactic, bribery. The ambassador offered Joseph Bonaparte and his younger brother Lucien 100,000 pounds—the equivalent of $25 million in modern dollars—if they would exert their powers of persuasion to keep Napoleon in an amicable frame of mind. Rumor had it that this offer escalated to 2 million pounds once Talleyrand scented the money and joined the conspiracy. The British government apparently thought it was still a bargain compared to the cost of a war.

This intrigue was not good news for the Americans. It meant that the first consul's plans for Santo Domingo and Louisiana would be pushed energetically by this influential trio as an alternative to war with the British. With the Floridas still unfortified and in the hands of the passive Spaniards, war with England would make Louisiana untenable for France. They could neither reinforce it nor supply it with the arms and ammunition needed for defense—presuming that General Victor's army got there intact.

Foreign Minister Talleyrand, delighted to find someone ready to pay him a fortune to sustain his wall of brass, was probably the most pleased of the three bribe takers. He prepared to devote his formidable gifts of persuasion, obfuscation, and backstairs treachery to keeping the first consul obsessed with making Louisiana a magnificent possession of imperial France.

10

The Big Bargain

In spite of his semideclaration of war, Napoleon seemingly continued to implement his plan to take possession of Louisiana. Pierre Clement de Laussat, the first consul's choice for prefect of the colony, had already sailed for New Orleans, assuming that General Victor and his army would soon follow him. Victor remained in the ice-choked Dutch port of Helvoet Sluys, mulling his orders to undermine the Americans with secret service money and Indian alliances.

But several things were going wrong with Napoleon's grand design. A British navy squadron began patrolling the waters off Helvoet Sluys to make sure that Victor's expedition did not turn into an invasion force destined for some point on the English or Scottish coast. In Spain, Secretary of State Madison's protest of the suspension of U.S. rights in New Orleans had produced a most unwelcome reaction, from the viewpoint of Bonaparte and Talleyrand. Their enemy, Manuel de Godoy, had persuaded King Carlos IV to restore the rights and send word of his change of heart to the Americans by the fastest ship in

Spain's service. Godoy had hedged his bet by making the restoration an act of personal generosity on the part of the king, leaving in abeyance the question of U.S. rights under the Treaty of 1795. Even so, it was not good news to the first consul and his foreign minister.

The Spanish had been encouraged to risk this act of defiance by the British ambassador to Madrid, who had informed them that his government had decided that Britain was not happy about France's acquisition of Louisiana. This British backing had also helped sustain Godoy in his struggle to prevent the king from ceding the Floridas to France. Louisiana had never been Spanish, Godoy argued, so there was no obloquy in relinquishing it. But Spain had discovered Florida and ruled it for two centuries. It was part of the national domain. The king's simple patriotism responded to this argument, persuading him to risk a Bonapartean thunderbolt.

Even worse news emanated from Santo Domingo. There General Donatien de Rochambeau, the new commander, was still fighting a sanguinary guerilla war. He had bought fifteen hundred bloodhounds (at $100 a dog) from English-owned Jamaica to hunt down the black freedom fighters, and had resorted to the most brutal, no-quarter tactics to terrorize the rebels. But the war continued to rage in the interior of the island. On Bonaparte's desk was an urgent request from Rochambeau for another thirty-five thousand men.

By this time, the mere idea of service in Santo Domingo sent shivers of fear through every regiment in the French army. The island was seen as a death trap; an estimated fifty thousand men had already died there of wounds or yellow fever. The island was also a desolated wreck, with plantations burned and their white owners refugees in Cap Francois and other port cities or in the United States. Many had fled to New Orleans, where their stories of torture and massacre had sent tremors of alarm through the local Creoles, who had a large slave population of their own to worry about.

Although Bonaparte's position as first consul seemed unassailable, ensconced in the Tuileries Palace, surrounded by the trappings of royalty, he was by no means as secure as he looked. The French army remained stubbornly republican. So did a large portion of the French people, who had voted against making him consul for life. A number of generals, including Bernadotte, had exhibited considerable dislike of Bonaparte's headstrong style and greed for power. Without the support of Police Minister Joseph Fouche, whose agents were everywhere detecting conspiracies, the first consul might have already become another victim of the devouring revolution.

Napoleon had rebounded from defeat in the past by turning in a new direction to win a victory. His failure in Egypt had been forgotten in the aftermath of Marengo. Was it time to do something similar in the aftermath of Santo Domingo? Even if he eventually conquered the island, it would take additional millions—money France did not have—to restore it. Meanwhile, he owned Louisiana at the expense of America's friendship—and without the Floridas he could not defend it against England's now overt hostility.

Chargé d'Affaires Pichon had supplied ample evidence of U.S. suspicion and opposition. Further evidence of that country's attitude reached Bonaparte from Robert R. Livingston early in April. The minister forwarded a copy of the New York *Chronicle*, which published the text of Senator Ross's resolutions calling for an immediate march on New Orleans by fifty thousand armed Americans. Around the same time the resolutions were also printed in a London newspaper, with gloating comments from the English editors about U.S. hostility to France. The paper was hastily forwarded to the first consul in a diplomatic pouch. Like the Federalists in the United States, the British also wryly speculated that the $2 million voted for Monroe's mission was intended for bribes.

For a while uncertainty tormented Bonaparte. He dispatched a vehement message to Lord Whitworth, claiming that General Victor's army had no intention of invading England; it was destined for Louisiana. He promised Rochambeau a reinforcement of fifteen thousand troops immediately and another fifteen thousand in the summer of 1803. But his mind, that powerful mix of intuition and instinct for self preservation, was already moving in another direction. There was a better way to rescue his military reputation than in a continuing pursuit of Talleyrand's dream of a colonial empire. There was too much of the *ancien regime* in that idea and perhaps too much of that annihilated era in Talleyrand as well. It was time to pursue a purely Bonapartean vision.

What would that be? Not Egypt or a war in distant India, which would be conducted by subordinate generals who might win too much glory for themselves. No, there was another choice—a lunge for the jugular of the one enemy Napoleon Bonaparte truly hated: England. He would make his next battle the invasion of perfidious Albion. He would dictate France's world supremacy in the ruins of London.

First, however, it was necessary to extricate himself from Louisiana. With his usual indifference to formalities, Bonaparte saw no need to await the arrival of Envoy Extraordinary Monroe. On Easter Sunday, April 10, 1803, Napoleon summoned Admiral Denis Decres, the minister of the navy, and Francois Barbe-Marbois, the minister of finance, to his country palace at St. Cloud outside Paris. There he stunned both men by announcing that he was thinking of selling Louisiana to the United States.

"I can hardly say I cede it to them," Napoleon admitted. "For it is not yet in our possession. [But] If I leave the least time to our enemies, I will transmit only an empty title to those republicans whose friendship I seek. They ask for only one town of Louisiana [New Orleans]; but I consider the whole colony as completely lost, and it seems to me that in the hands of that growing power, it will be more useful to the policy and even the commerce of France than if I should try to keep it."

Crusty Admiral Decres, who had spent much of the previous year shipping men to Santo Domingo and planning naval bases in Florida and New Orleans, vehemently protested the first consul's proposal. He said France would never have a navy if she abandoned her colonies. "It does not become you to fear the kings of England," he said in his blunt way.

But Marbois, who had already devoted several years of his life to allying France with the United States, was in complete agreement with Napoleon's idea. "We should not hesitate to make a sacrifice of that which is slipping from us," he said. "War with England is inevitable."

The next morning, Napoleon called the finance minister to the palace again and told him he had made up his mind. "Irresolution and deliberation are no longer in season," Bonaparte said. "I renounce Louisiana. It is not only New Orleans I cede, but the whole colony, without reserve."

The first consul declared he had made the decision "with the greatest regret." He had demonstrated how important he considered the province by the time and effort he had devoted to persuading the Spaniards to cede it to France. But trying to retain it now would be "folly."

"I direct you to negotiate this affair," Napoleon said. "Do not even wait for the arrival of Mr. Monroe; have an interview this day with Mr. Livingston. I require a great deal of money for this war [with England]. I want 50 million francs—for less than that sum I will not treat."

That same day, April 11, Foreign Minister Talleyrand summoned the U.S. minister to his residence on the Rue du Bac and almost casually asked him if he would be interested in buying all of Louisiana. The thunderstruck Livingston said no. He reminded Talleyrand what he had been repeating for a year—that the United States only wanted New Orleans and the Floridas, and possibly, if France was willing, the territory north of the Arkansas River.

Talleyrand replied that if they surrendered New Orleans, the rest of the territory was virtually useless to France. He wanted to know what the United States would give for the whole thing. Realizing that the foreign minister was more or less serious, Livingston suggested 20 million francs—$4 million—provided France also agreed to pay the claims of U.S. merchants.

That was much too low, Talleyrand replied. He suggested that Livingston think it over and contact him tomorrow. The minister replied that James Monroe had landed at Le Havre and was en route to Paris. He preferred to wait until his colleague arrived, possibly with fresh instructions from Washington. After Monroe was officially introduced to Talleyrand, Livingston assured him that they would be glad to discuss the proposition in more detail.

Talleyrand shrugged and said he was not authorized to discuss the subject. The idea had just "struck him" as a good one. The foreign minister's network of private informants had apparently tipped him off about Bonaparte's decision, and Talleyrand was trying to get into the game for gain or glory—more likely a little of both.

Monroe landed at Le Havre on April 8, 1803. The special envoy immediately dispatched a letter to Livingston, telling him he was in France at last. Livingston's reply, written on April 10, was anything but optimistic. After congratulating Monroe on his safe arrival, the minister wrote: "God grant that your mission may answer yours and the public's expectations. War may do something for us. Nothing else will." Livingston's only other hope was the possibility that Monroe was bringing news of the U.S. seizure of New Orleans. Then "we should do well" in any future negotiations.

His pessimism having been abolished by Talleyrand's April 11 offer, Livingston suddenly realized he might cut a deal that would make Monroe superfluous. The next day he returned to Talleyrand's residence on the Rue du Bac for a maddening conversation with the devious ex-Bishop of Autun. Talleyrand maintained that his proposition was "only personal," but he still wanted Livingston to make a reasonable offer. When Livingston again declined, Talleyrand shrugged his shoulders and changed the subject.

Unaware of Napoleon's order to Marbois, or of Whitworth's bribe, Livingston could not penetrate Talleyrand's game. The foreign minister was either hoping to get an offer that would top the figure Marbois obtained, thus making him look superior to the finance minister, or to muddy the waters so thoroughly that the negotiation would fall through, forcing Napoleon to cancel his plans for war with England. That in turn would enable Talleyrand to demand more pounds sterling from Lord Whitworth.

Flailing in an information vacuum, Livingston suggested that he write a letter to Secretary of State Madison, which Talleyrand would send to Washington via General Bernadotte. The letter would state that Talleyrand "in reply to my various notes" had been directed to ask him to begin a negotiation—in this case for Louisiana. The ploy was graphic evidence of how desperate Livingston was to claim all the credit for winning Louisiana. The French foreign minister coyly replied he would have to answer that proposal evasively "because Louisiana was not theirs."

Livingston grew more than a little excited. He told Talleyrand that he had seen a copy of the treaty with Spain.

He, along with everyone else in Paris, knew that the first consul had appointed civil officers to govern the province and that General Victor had orders to take possession of it. Still Talleyrand insisted that France had not obtained Louisiana. Strictly speaking, he was correct. Until Pierre Laussat arrived in New Orleans and officially took charge of the colony, Louisiana was still in Spanish hands.

In that case, Livingston replied, he would try to persuade Mr. Monroe to join him in recommending to the U.S. government an immediate seizure of New Orleans from Spain by force. They had ample reason to justify such a move. The minister warned Talleyrand that he and Monroe "were not disposed to trifle" any longer in this maddening matter. When Monroe arrived, Livingston was sure that they would have instructions from Secretary of State Madison demanding a "precise & prompt" decision.

Revealing his jealousy of Monroe, the minister added that he did not want to go home with a reputation as "an indolent negotiator." Talleyrand laughed and said he would give him a certificate stating that he was the "most importunate" diplomat he had ever encountered. As Livingston left Talleyrand's splendid house on the Rue du Bac, he must have felt like a man wandering in a labyrinth, searching for a clue that would tell him where he was going.

Later that same day, April 12, James Monroe and his family arrived in Paris. Livingston welcomed them cordially. They were old acquaintances from revolutionary days. While the Livingston women made their female counterparts comfortable in the U.S. embassy, Monroe and Livingston spent several hours in conversation. The special envoy read Livingston's various letters and memorials to Talleyrand as well as the foreign minister's evasive replies, and listened to Livingston's report of his recent conversation with Talleyrand about buying all of Louisiana.

Toward evening, the two families and several guests sat down to dinner. In the middle of the meal, Livingston spotted François Barbe-Marbois strolling up and down in the embassy garden. The minister sent one of his sons-in-law to invite him to join them. The finance minister said he would come back when they finished dining. Marbois returned while they were sipping their coffee and after some general conversation Livingston took him into an adjoining room.

The U.S. minister promptly told Marbois about Talleyrand's strange performance. Marbois was extremely interested and said the foreign minister's behavior could be explained by something that was under discussion at St. Cloud. But Marbois did not think it was a good idea to go into it at that time, with the embassy full of company. The finance minister asked Livingston to visit him later that night at his office in the French Treasury.

When Monroe expressed a desire to join the conference, Livingston's animosity toward the special envoy's appointment surfaced unmistakably. The minister said that would offend diplomatic propriety because Monroe had not yet been officially presented to Foreign Minister Talleyrand. This legalism left Monroe in a very perturbed state of mind. His mood was not improved by information that he had already obtained from a "confidential friend" about Napoleon's decision to sell Louisiana.

Livingston hurried off to Marbois' office, hoping to buy Louisiana from a man he trusted. Marbois had a reputation for integrity—the total opposite of Talleyrand. The finance minister also spoke excellent English, making it easy for Livingston to converse with him.

Marbois, no slouch at negotiating on behalf of his country, proceeded to concoct a fictional version of his talk with Napoleon. He reported that Bonaparte had told him, "You have charge of the treasury. Let them give you a hundred million francs and pay their own claims and take the whole country [of Louisiana]." Marbois was asking for $25 million. He tried to soften this blow by pointing out that at least 20 percent—over $5 million—would go to settle U.S. claims against France.

Livingston pretended to blanch at this astronomical price, which was still a bargain for 838,000 square miles of land. He protested that the figure was much too high and reiterated that the United States only wanted to buy New Orleans and the Floridas. He did not mention that he and Monroe were authorized to pay as much as $10 million for this mere fringe of North America.

Marbois tried to turn the tables by persuading Livingston to name a figure. When the minister remained coy—a year of taking lessons in evasion from Talleyrand may have helped him considerably here—the finance minister dropped his price to 60 million francs—$15 million—with $5 million included for U.S. claims.

Concealing his inner exultation, Livingston solemnly told Marbois that "it was vain to ask for anything that was so greatly beyond our means." Marbois coolly reminded

Livingston that the United States, with its excellent credit, could easily borrow the money. Livingston pretended to remain unconvinced. He warned Marbois that if the Jefferson administration paid such a price, they would lose the next election and restore the French-hating Federalists to power. At midnight he departed, saying that he would consult with Monroe, but he was certain neither of them would agree to the price the finance minister was asking.

Back in his residence, Livingston devoted almost three hours to writing a long letter to James Madison, hoping to get on the record that he had all but bought Louisiana without any help from James Monroe. To the secretary of state, the ambassador had no hesitation in crowing over the bargain. The value of the land alone would more than repay the price, even if they had to "go the sum" proposed by Marbois. Livingston claimed that he was rushing the letter by the first available ship because he wanted to "calm the tumult" in the United States that the news of the war between France and England was likely to arouse. But the final sentence, written at 3 A.M., contained the real purpose of his dispatch. "We shall do all we can to cheapen the purchase, but my present sentiment is we shall buy."

11
Hanging Fire

The following day, April 14, 1803, special envoy Monroe was presented to Foreign Minister Talleyrand, making his status official. On April 15, the two Americans began bargaining with Marbois. On the surface the envoys seemed to be in agreement, but they were far from a harmonious team. That same day Monroe wrote a lugubrious letter to Madison, complaining about Livingston.

The "confidential friend" who had told Monroe about Louisiana being in play was Fulwar Skipwith, the American commercial agent in Paris. He had been Monroe's colleague during his disastrous 1794–1796 tour as minister—and contributed not a little to his misjudgments. Skipwith filled fellow Virginian Monroe's ears with tales of the way Livingston had been working day and night "to turn the occurrences in America and even my mission to his account."

Apparently, Skipwith thought—and Monroe agreed—that Livingston should have retired into the silence the moment he heard of Monroe's appointment. The envoy extraordinary found confirmation of this supposed back-stabbing in his perusal of Livingston's correspondence, which the New Yorker had permitted him to read without reserve. Monroe complained that the letters proved "that he did not abstain, even when he heard I was on my way, from the topics entrusted to us jointly."

Skipwith also told Monroe that Livingston had vocally "regretted his misfortune" because the special envoy's arrival deprived him of the credit for settling matters. The commercial agent had been one of the guests at the dinner party on April 12, and Livingston's refusal to let Monroe accompany him to Marbois' office had filled Skipwith with righteous indignation. It was the opening round of an ugly quarrel about who deserved credit for buying Louisiana.

For a week the two Americans sparred with Marbois about the price, apparently oblivious to the possibility that delay might wreck the negotiation. Behind the scenes, there was powerful opposition to Napoleon's decision. Admiral Decres was by no means the only significant figure who thought Bonaparte was displaying timidity by disposing of Louisiana before the British even declared war. General Bernadotte, a potential rival for supreme power, was reportedly of the same opinion.

Even more distressed was the trio that British ambassador Lord Whitworth had bribed to prolong the Peace of Amiens. Talleyrand had no difficulty convincing Joseph Bonaparte that Louisiana was the hinge on which swung peace or war. Cupidity was not the foreign minister's only motive. He sincerely wanted to see France regain her lost colonial glory—and even more voraciously hungered for his wall of brass to confine the pushy Americans to the eastern seaboard.

Joseph swiftly persuaded Lucien Bonaparte to join him in opposition. Lucien had negotiated the treaty of San Idelfonso, winning Louisiana's retrocession. That gave him a personal claim to the policy of colonial glory. Whitworth's pounds sterling only added to his passion. Another motive may have been the bribe he extracted from witless King Carlos IV during his brief ambassadorship: no less than 5 million francs, plus a treasure trove of paintings by old masters.

Early one morning at the end of the week of inconclusive negotiations, Joseph and Lucien paid a visit to the Tuileries Palace. The found their brother in his bath, but this inconvenience did not prevent the first consul from seeing them. Napoleon, perhaps guessing why they had come, asked Lucien what he thought of his decision to sell Louisiana.

Lucien replied that "The Chambers"—the three branches of the French legislature, which Napoleon kept in business to provide pro forma approval of his decrees—would not approve of it. Joseph emphatically seconded Lucien's opinion, noting that he had already warned Napoleon that there was serious opposition among the legislators.

"And what did I answer?" Napoleon growled.

"That you would do it without the chambers," Joseph glumly replied.

"Precisely!" Napoleon snapped. "That is what I have taken the great liberty to tell Mr. Joseph and what I now repeat to Citizen Lucien—begging him to give me his opinion about it, without taking into consideration his paternal tenderness for his diplomatic conquest."

When neither brother spoke, Napoleon defied them to their faces. "Think of it what you will. Both of you go into mourning about this affair. I shall do [it] without the consent of anyone whatsoever. Do you understand?"

Infuriated by this arrogance, Joseph lost his temper and shouted that he was prepared to lead the opposition in the legislature. "I am not fond of mounting the tribune [but] this time you will see me there!"

Napoleon half rose from his tub to shout that there would be no opposition to lead. "There will be no debate!" The sale of Louisiana would be "negotiated by me, shall be ratified and executed by me alone, do you comprehend?—by me, who laugh at your opposition!"

Losing all semblance of self control, Joseph advanced to the edge of the tub to bellow that he would still lead the opposition, even if it meant that they would join the republican opponents Napoleon had "so legally, so humanely" transported to exile in French Guyana.

"You are insolent!" Napoleon roared. "I ought—"

In his rage, he threw himself backward in the tub, sending a cascade of perfumed water into Joseph's face. The first consul's valet, Constant, fainted, fearing he was about to witness a replay of the murder in his tub of a leader of the reign of terror, Jean Paul Marat. Joseph, drenched to the skin, stammered oaths, his hands working, on the brink of apoplexy if not murder.

Lucien rescued the situation with a mocking quote from

Virgil. The words, in the mouth of the god Neptune, were apropos: "But better it is to calm the troubled waves; hereafter it is not with a penalty like this that you will pay for your misdeeds."

Perhaps mollified by this comparison to a god, Napoleon summoned servants to dry off Joseph, who went home to change his clothes. Lucien remained while Napoleon began dressing and persisted in arguing against selling Louisiana. Abruptly the Man of Destiny admitted: "I am more sorry than I like to confess for the expedition to Santo Domingo."

They debated what Napoleon called his "Louisianacide," mocking Lucien's view of the decision. Finally, Lucien also lost his temper, forgetting his status as a heretofore dutiful, if somewhat erratic, younger brother. He said the sale was "unconstitutional."

This drew a sarcastic laugh from Napoleon. Lucien, the manipulator of plebiscites, was hardly the man to revere the constitution. "You lay it on handsomely," he said. "Unconstitutional is droll from you."

"Citizen Consul," Lucien said. "If I were not your brother I would be your enemy."

"My enemy!" Napoleon roared. "My enemy! . . . You my enemy! I would break you like this box!" he yelled, seizing a snuffbox from a nearby dresser and smashing it into fragments on the floor.

Lucien retreated, but neither he nor Joseph abandoned the argument. They staged several more violent scenes over the next several days as the negotiations over Louisiana continued. At one point, according to Lucien, the first consul became so alarmed at Joseph's wrath that he retreated to Josephine's boudoir.

Both men sensed that Louisiana was a turning point in Napoleon's career. Having wrested mastery of Europe from England, they saw him as needlessly seeking war again—a war that they feared France would not win. Louisiana, the prize Napoleon had acquired without firing a shot, was an example of what could be accomplished by astute diplomacy and the threat of France's military might. All the Bonapartes, including the first consul, were on their way to becoming fabulously rich. Why risk everything for another gamble on the god of battles?

Oblivious to this pressure on Napoleon to revoke his offer, Livingston and Monroe let the negotiations sink into a total stall, hoping that Marbois would lower his price. Although they agreed between themselves to pay as much as 50 million francs, they declined to go above 40 million. Marbois, knowing Napoleon could change his mind, reported that the first consul had reacted "coldly" to this offer. The finance minister hinted that the negotiation might be taken out of his hands at any moment, which would mean dealing with Talleyrand. The threat inspired the Americans to boost their offer to 50 million francs.

Marbois warned that if Napoleon rejected this figure, the whole *projet* might collapse. This was something less than the truth; 50 million was the first consul's original asking price. Marbois was probably trying to extract a higher offer, but he also may have been reflecting what he undoubtedly knew about the many objections to the sale.

French patriots such as Decres and bribe takers such as

Joseph and Lucien Bonaparte were not the only opposition. In talkative Paris, secrets were hard to keep. If the Spanish learned that Napoleon was violating his solemn promise to return Louisiana to them rather than yield it to a third party, they could and probably would raise a huge uproar. They might be doing it at this very moment through Talleyrand, who was not above leaking the double cross to them.

Still confident that they had hooked the whale, Livingston and Monroe decided "to rest for a few days on our oars." Monroe conveniently developed back trouble, which sent him to bed. On April 23, the impatient Marbois went to Monroe's lodgings with two written proposals. Livingston joined them there and tough bargaining resumed, with Monroe reclining on a sofa to rest his back.

Marbois began by reporting he had been appointed a minister plenipotentiary, with full powers to negotiate a treaty. His first proposal was supposedly from Napoleon, and made extravagant demands—America would have to favor French commerce in New Orleans indefinitely—and the asking price was the astronomical hundred million francs Marbois had demanded in his first talk with Livingston.

When the Americans demurred, Marbois produced a draft of a treaty, drawn by himself, which gave France and Spain limited commercial privileges in New Orleans and arranged for settling U.S. claims. He said he "thought" Napoleon would accept it—and asked the Americans to name a price. Livingston and Monroe took Marbois's proposals back to their residences and each made some changes in the section dealing with U.S. claims.

On April 29, the two Americans called on Marbois at

the treasury to discuss their proposed changes, which he found acceptable. The envoys offered 50 million francs plus 20 million for the claims. Marbois politely but very firmly said that if they did not raise their offer to 60 million francs, negotiations were *fini*. The Americans, perhaps exchanging uneasy glances (after all, there was nothing in their instructions that authorized them to spend so much money) agreed to 60 million francs for Louisiana and 20 million for the claims, bringing the total price up to $20 million.

A delighted Marbois took the offer to Napoleon at St. Cloud the next morning. While nothing official was said, it soon became apparent that a deal had been struck. On May 1, Monroe and Livingston were invited to the Tuileries, where they dined with Bonaparte. The Man of Destiny said not a word about Louisiana beyond remarking that he hoped that the negotiation would be settled soon. This terse remark was probably another way of warning the Americans not to drag their feet any longer. It also reflected Napoleon's eagerness to get his hands on the Americans' cash.

That night, Monroe and Livingston met with Marbois at his office, and the finance minister told them that the first consul had agreed to the terms. By now the Americans had become aware that the prize might slip away from them. Livingston's numerous contacts in the diplomatic corps may have told him about the pressure on Napoleon from Talleyrand and the brothers Bonaparte. Even more alarming was the drift to war with England, raising the specter of an English seizure of the territory.

The British had made it clear to Minister Rufus King that they were now determined to prevent Napoleon from occupying Louisiana. At one point they told King that they were ready to dispatch a fleet and army to occupy the province. The doughty King had strenuously informed them that George III's army and navy would be even more unacceptable in New Orleans than Bonaparte's legions.

Some large questions remained unanswered, in particular the exact boundaries of Louisiana. When the Americans asked Marbois to clarify this rather vital point, he went to Napoleon, who curtly declined to help. "If an obscurity did not already exist, it would perhaps be good policy to put one there," he told the finance minister.

It was an interesting glimpse of the game that the first consul was playing in his head. From Napoleon's point of view, there was not a trace of friendship for the United States in this transaction. If anything, he hoped that in the not-too-distant future, when he had disposed of England, he would have the power to raise all sorts of difficult questions about Louisiana, not excluding the unpardonable affront to his ally, Spain, and perhaps declare that the sale was void.

Another idea in play was Secretary of State Madison's statement to Chargé d'Affaires Pichon that if Americans went west of the Mississippi, they would eventually secede from the federal government and create a separate state. Napoleon found this possibility fascinating. He saw himself tampering with the loyalty of this new nation, turning them into a French satellite, hostile to Washington, D.C. The first consul all but rubbed his hands in gleeful anticipation of this future maneuver. "We must expect rivalries in the bosom of the Union," he told Marbois. "Confederations which are called perpetual last only until one of the contracting parties finds it to its interest to break them."

Further evidence of French hostility came from Talleyrand when Livingston rushed to him to ask if he would be good enough to pinpoint the eastern boundary of Louisiana. Surely, said the American minister, the orders to General Victor included some specific geographical realities. In fact, Victor's orders had specified that Louisiana extended south all the way to the Rio Grande—meaning it included present day Texas. But Talleyrand, with a copy of the orders on his desk, ineffably replied: "I do not know. You must take it [Louisiana] as you received it."

The baffled Livingston asked if this meant the Americans could "construe [the boundaries] our own way?"

With unmistakable venom, the foreign minister snapped: "I can give you no directions. You have made a noble bargain for yourselves, and I suppose you will make the most of it."

Livingston persuaded Monroe to resolve the boundary problem by putting into the treaty the exact wording of the Treaty of San Idelfonso, in which Spain ceded Louisiana to France. Unfortunately, there was no mention of boundaries in this statement. But Livingston had been frantically researching old maps and documents, and he had concluded that there were good grounds for claiming Louisiana included West Florida between the Mississippi and Perdido Rivers. Monroe agreed with this claim, which would complete U.S. control of both banks of the

Mississippi to its mouth. But neither man was disposed to waste time arguing the point with Marbois or Talleyrand.

The Americans made a halfhearted attempt to insert into the treaty a promise that the first consul would use his good offices to persuade Spain to relinquish the Floridas. But Napoleon refused to approve it, saying he would only offer them his verbal promise, which in the light of what we know now, was worse than worthless.

The Americans abandoned the boundary question to future negotiations with Spain and France, relying on the quotation from the Treaty of San Idelfonso. As Monroe put it in a letter, the main thing was: "We must not lose time."

The envoys gave even less attention to the wording of how the claims against France would be settled. Monroe, whose abilities as a legal thinker were not great, added a clause muddling future negotiations with problems already settled in the Treaty of Mortefontaine. Worse, both men allowed the French government to have the final word—a mistake when the arbiter of that final word would be the notoriously corrupt Talleyrand.

Finally, at Marbois' insistence, they accepted a clause in the treaty that specified that the inhabitants of Louisiana would be incorporated into the American union as soon as possible and accorded "all the rights, advantages and immunities of citizens of the United States." Secretary of State Madison had instructed Monroe to avoid such an agreement if they succeeded in buying New Orleans and the Floridas.

Livingston later excused these gaffes by attesting to the Americans' sense of urgency: "The moment was critical," he told Madison. "The question of peace or war was in the balance; and it was important to come to a conclusion."

On May 2, in Finance Minister Marbois's office, the two Americans signed the treaty. It was written in French, which both of them read fairly well. An English translation was promised in a day or two. By this time, both envoys knew that they had achieved something epochal. "We have lived long," Livingston is reported to have said. "But this is the noblest work of our whole lives."

Monroe was equally pleased with the achievement, if not with his negotiating partner. His euphoria was evident in a letter to Marbois in which he said that the Frenchman's role in the negotiation added "not a little to the gratification which I derive from the event." Marbois was an "old friend" who had experienced with him the "extraordinary movements of the epoch in which we live."

Napoleon Bonaparte was also delighted. "The negotiations leave me nothing to wish," he chortled to Marbois. "Sixty million for an occupation that will not last perhaps a day! I want France to have the good of this unexpected capital."

The first consul called in a secretary and dictated an order to devote the Louisiana windfall to building five canals to improve French commerce. Finance Minister Marbois went away even more impressed with a man he frequently described as a genius. But Bonaparte's performance was window dressing, to mollify or divert some of the still angry French opposition to the sale. Not a franc was ever spent on the canals. Every single one of the 60 million francs went into the preparations for the invasion of England.

Finance Minister Marbois had no difficulty arranging the monetary details of the sale. When news of the deal reached London, the British government decided that U.S. possession of Louisiana was the lesser of the two evils and permitted one of their premier banks, Baring Brothers, to join Amsterdam's Hope and Company in floating the loan that would give Napoleon his money with the rapidity he desired. The bankers were eager to cooperate; their commission on the deal was almost $3 million.

Within two weeks, England and France were at war. British orders went out to its battle fleet to attack any and all French ships on the high seas, claiming that Napoleon's refusal to evacuate The Netherlands had broken the Treaty of Amiens. Bonaparte called the British Navy a despicable swarm of pirates. But he made a point of announcing the ratification of the sale of Louisiana on the same day he declared that hostilities had been renewed. The first consul candidly admitted that he did not "want to leave any ground for considering the colony as still French."

One large question remained unanswered: What would President Thomas Jefferson and Secretary of State James Madison think of this deal, which made mincemeat of their instructions to Envoy Extraordinary Monroe? How would they fit the acquisition of this vast territory into the Republican Party's strict interpretation of the Constitution, which said not a word about such an event?

12

Constitution Bending in Washington, D.C.

In Washington, D.C., during the same momentous month of April, President Jefferson was preparing for the worst. On April 8, the day that Livingston forwarded to Talleyrand and Napoleon the newspaper containing the Ross resolutions, the president asked his five-man cabinet to vote on whether the United States should seek an alliance with England if France persisted in its plan to occupy Louisiana. The cabinet voted 3–2 in favor of such a move, and Madison soon drafted new instructions to Monroe and Livingston, allowing Monroe to feel free to go to London and negotiate with the British if the French proved obdurate.

Nothing better demonstrated the president's growing desperation than this flirtation with the country he had denounced for the previous decade as the source of all political evil. He continued to demonstrate his new tilt publicly for the benefit of Chargé Andre Pichon by being excessively attentive to British Chargé Edward Thornton at White House dinners. He even told Thornton that if American relations with France continued to deteriorate, the United States would "throw away the scabbard," and declare war. Thornton responded to this remark by sending Envoy Extraordinary Monroe a letter of introduction to Lord Whitworth, to facilitate his obtaining a passport to England.

Almost three months had passed since Monroe's appointment. The Mississippi was still closed to U.S. commerce and the Federalist press was gloating over Jefferson's hesitation and timidity. Then came news that was received in Washington, D.C. with exorbitant exultation. Spanish Ambassador Yrujo presented Secretary of State Madison with a message from Madrid, ordering Intendant Morales to restore U.S. privileges in New Orleans. The secretary swiftly arranged for the message to be published in the newspapers.

Jefferson embraced the news as a diplomatic triumph of gigantic proportions. In four months, the president declared, the United States had gained what they wanted and needed from Spain by peaceful diplomacy. "To have seized N. Orleans as our federal maniacs wished," he said, would have cost $100 million and one hundred thousand lives.

Few realistic Americans—or anyone else in the world— would have agreed with the president's estimate of the cost of a war with enfeebled Spain. The governor of the Mississippi Territory had already told Jefferson that he could capture New Orleans from the Spaniards with six hundred militiamen. Moreover, when Secretary of State Madison examined the message from Spain, he was underwhelmed. He quickly noted that the Spanish said they were restoring U.S. privileges in New Orleans as an act of benevolence on the part of the king. There was no concession whatsoever to the U.S. claim that they had a right to export their goods and produce through the city based on the 1795 treaty with Spain. The king's act easily could be construed as a delaying action, enabling the French to do as they pleased when they occupied the city.

Nevertheless, the news of the restoration had a calming effect on the angry men of the West. Thereafter, for almost two months, there was only a suspenseful silence from Europe. In late June the midnight letter that Livingston had written on April 13 reached Washington, telling the president and his secretary of state that France was offering all of Louisiana. Madison immediately responded with a letter authorizing the two envoys to make the purchase.

"The dawn of your negotiations has given much pleasure and much expectation," wrote Madison. Purchasing Louisiana had not been considered "within the frame of probability" when Monroe sailed to France. Madison advised the envoys to tell the French that there need be no doubt that the United States would support the purchase, even though it exceeded the envoys' original instructions.

The news that Louisiana had become part of the United States was first announced by the Boston *Independent Chronicle* on June 30, 1803. "LOUISIANA CEDED TO THE UNITED STATES!" shouted the headline. The news spread throughout the rest of the country as fast as ships and post riders could carry it. The glad tidings reached

Washington, D.C., on July 3, in a letter from retiring minister Rufus King, who had just arrived in New York from London. King enclosed a letter that Monroe and Livingston had written to him before he sailed, reporting their triumph.

The secretary of state rushed King's letter to Jefferson at the White House. He rushed it to Samuel Harrison Smith, editor of the *National Intelligencer*, which had become the administration's semiofficial newspaper. The next morning, citizens from the new federal city and the surrounding Maryland and Virginia countryside thronged to the White House for an Independence Day celebration. At about noon, Jefferson appeared on the steps of the mansion, surrounded by his cabinet, and had the exquisite pleasure of announcing the good news while copies of the *Intelligencer* were passed from hand to hand, describing the bargain in more detail.

That same day, Jefferson's secretary, Captain Meriwether Lewis, left the White House to rendezvous with his partner, Lieutenant William Clark, and begin their exploration of Louisiana. Jefferson had shared Livingston's midnight letter of April 13 with Lewis, and on June 21 he had informed Clark of his "very sanguine expectations" that the territory would be the property of the United States in less than a year. The news that the sale had been consummated excited Lewis so much that he forgot his wallet. When he returned to get it, he spent an hour in conversation with the exultant president about the new importance of his expedition.

That Fourth of July, the *Intelligencer* declared, was a

proud day for President Jefferson. The newspaper gave him all the credit for the astonishingly successful negotiation. "We have secured our rights by pacific means," the *Intelligencer*'s editor wrote. "Truth and reason have been more powerful than the sword." This editorial comment was mild compared to the crowing of the Boston *Independent Chronicle*. "The wise, seasonable and politic negotiation of the President, approved and confirmed by Congress, has gloriously terminated to the immortal honor of the friends of peace and good government and to the utter disappointment of the factious and turbulent throughout the Union." This back of the hand to the Federalist call for war became the leitmotif of the Jeffersonian republican view of the Louisiana Purchase.

The Federalists took a very different stance toward the sale. George Cabot, one of the leaders of the party in New England, told Rufus King that he thought it was "like selling us a ship that is surrounded by the British fleet." France had rid herself of an "encumbrance" that was wounding her pride, and was getting a great deal of money for it. Another Federalist complained in mid-July 1803, "We are to give money of which we have too little for land of which we already have too much." Fisher Ames, the most eloquent of the Federalists, saw America "rushing like a comet into infinite space."

Moreover, Louisiana was "a great waste," a wilderness unpeopled with any beings except wolves and wandering Indians. That meant it could be "cut up into states without number, but each with *two votes in the Senate*." Worst of all, these new states would be loyal to "imperial Virginia."

The home state of Jefferson, Madison, and Monroe would "be confirmed in her claim of dominion over the rest of the states."

Worse, the inhabitants of these new "mountaineer states" would "claim power and resist taxes." Were not the Kentuckians in the national legislature plague enough for one country? Now "other like thickskinned beasts will crowd Congress Hall—buffaloes from the head of the Missouri and alligators from the Red River."

An exception to this Federalist opposition to the purchase was the voice of General Alexander Hamilton in the *New York Evening Post.* Hamilton praised the acquisition of the territory. From the beginning of his career as a politician, the general had labored to fulfill his vision of the United States as a future world power. But he declined to give Jefferson any credit for this great leap forward. "Every man possessed of the least candour and reflection," he wrote, would admit that the happy result was achieved by "unforeseen and unexpected circumstances" rather than any "wise or vigorous measures" on the part of the U.S. government. The best explanation was "the kind interpositions of an over-ruling Providence."

The Federalists became even more exercised when the details of the treaty—especially the $15,000,000 purchase price—became known. (The $5,000,000 for U.S. claims against France evoked no protests because many of the claimants were Federalists.) The Boston *Columbian Centinel* cried that "THE ADDITION OF LOUISIANA IS ONLY A PRETENCE FOR DRAWING AN IMMENSE SUM OF MONEY FROM US" which can only be viewed as "a contribution to the support of a power [already] too great for the safety and liberty of the civilized world."

The Federalist editors' imaginations worked overtime to impress on their readers the size of the U.S. payment. Fifteen million dollars was the equivalent of 433 tons of solid silver. It would fill 866 wagons, which would make a wagon train five and one-third miles long. Stacked in dollars, it would make a pile nine miles high. It would pay each soldier in an army of 40,000 men $10 a week for 40 years. Divided among the citizens it would give every man, woman, and child in the county $3 each.

At the heart of this hullabaloo was the bitter fact that the Federalist Party had largely dwindled to the New England states. The 1802 congressional elections had been another triumph for the Republicans. They now controlled the House of Representatives, 103–29 and the Senate by 25–9. The descendants of the Puritans feared that the acquisition of Louisiana, which would double the size of the United States, meant they would soon become an impotent minority in the councils of the nation. This future was hard if not impossible for these proud Yankees to accept. They saw themselves as the creators of the nation, thanks to the heroes who fought at Lexington, Concord, and Bunker Hill.

Intermixed with this fear of insignificance was a genuine revulsion against Napoleonic France, which the Federalists accurately saw as a dictatorship that was the enemy of free societies everywhere. To help fund Bonaparte's war machine seemed immoral, no matter how patent the advantages to the United States.

Another quarrel that soon preoccupied the newspaper editors was the competition between Robert R. Livingston and James Monroe over who deserved credit for the purchase. Livingston did not help his own cause by trying to elbow Monroe out of the limelight. He arranged for friends in the United States to publish his 1802 memorial to Talleyrand in which he argued that Louisiana was a costly boondoggle for France that would never pay a franc on the millions it would require to develop the territory. It appeared in the newspapers with a laudatory introduction from an unnamed American in Paris.

Livingston also tried to backdate when he heard about Napoleon's decision to sell, so that it occurred before Monroe arrived at Le Havre. He proceeded to put this fiction into letters to numerous friends in the United States. Combined with the memorial, it made him look like the sole weaver of the spell that convinced the first consul to part with the prize. But Livingston could not obliterate the date on which he sent the electrifying news to Madison in his midnight letter—the day Monroe arrived in Paris.

Monroe's friends retaliated, with the covert help of the special envoy, by publishing the despondent letter that Livingston had written to Monroe when he reached Le Havre, informing him that only a war could rescue the situation. Publicly, Monroe took an opposite tack. In a letter addressed to Virginia's senators he humbly denied any special credit for the purchase. Napoleon's decision to sell was the result of President Jefferson's masterful diplomacy, of which Monroe's mission was only the most conspicuous feature. All he would claim by way of credit was "the pronounced character which I had in reference to the object in question"—his known desire to avoid a war with France and to vindicate the right of the western Americans to use the Mississippi.

Not surprisingly, Jefferson and Madison sided emphatically with their self-effacing fellow Virginian. On July 30, 1803, Madison wrote a pungent letter to Monroe about the circulation of Livingston's memorial in the newspapers. He said it made Livingston look like "Magnus Apollo" and was so "improper" it was hard to believe the minister had authorized it. Madison agreed with Monroe that Livingston should have remained silent after he learned of the special envoy's appointment. The secretary of state thought that if the appeal to the French had been "less hackneyed" by Livingston, and made by the two of them "under the solemnity of a joint and extraordinary embassy," the treaty might have been more advantageous to the United States. This patently partisan argument is, to say the least, debatable.

Behind these sharp words were some large political considerations. There were strong rumors that Livingston was hoping his achievement would entitle him to replace Aaron Burr as vice president when Jefferson ran for reelection in 1804. That might make the New Yorker a candidate for president in 1808. Both Madison and Monroe had thoughts in this same ambitious direction.

Also in the newspapers was some messy business with Edward Livingston, the minister's younger brother. He was not only mayor of New York City; the president had also appointed him federal attorney for the empire state. In the summer of 1803, Livingston discovered that a clerk in his office had embezzled a huge sum of money. When he asked the Jefferson administration for a stay on repaying the loss, the answer was a stony no. Livingston had been forced to sell virtually everything he owned to pay the debt. Bitterly denouncing the president as an ingrate, Edward headed for a city that offered a man a second chance to succeed: New Orleans.

Meanwhile, by mid-July President Jefferson and Secretary of State Madison had received the text of the Louisiana treaty and were pondering some of its troublesome aspects. Jefferson had campaigned for president as a proponent of a strict interpretation of the Constitution. He and the Old Republicans in his party believed that this policy was the only safeguard against letting the federal government acquire dangerous amounts of arbitrary power. They had passionately denounced the argument of Alexander Hamilton and other Federalists that there were implied powers in the Constitution that entitled the government to take action in areas not covered in the text of the national charter.

On July 16, the president convened a cabinet meeting and told his colleagues that he thought the Constitution would have to be amended to bring Louisiana into the union. He had already drafted a possible amendment, which he circulated to the five secretaries. It was a long, complicated affair that would have divided Louisiana between white and Indian inhabitants.

At the cabinet meeting the president discovered that no one thought much of this legislative effort. The department heads pointed out that the treaty stipulated both sides had to ratify it in six months. This deadline meant that the United States should sign it by October 30. (Although signed on May 2, the treaty was dated April 30.) Getting an amendment to the Constitution approved in such a tight time frame was manifestly impossible.

Jefferson admitted the force of this argument; Congress was not scheduled to meet until late November. He decided to call a special session for October 17 to win Senate approval of the treaty and persuade the House of Representatives to vote the money for it within the deadline. He also took the first step toward occupying Louisiana. He ordered William C. C. Claiborne, who was already on the border as governor of the Mississippi Territory, and General James Wilkinson, the commander of the U.S. army, to prepare to take possession of New Orleans.

These decisions did not stop Jefferson from fretting over the constitutionality of the acquisition. In August he wrote to Senator John Breckinridge of Kentucky, known to be a constitutional purist, and flatly declared that the national charter had made no provision for acquiring foreign territory. But this "fugitive occurrence"—Napoleon's decision to sell Louisiana—so manifestly "advances the good of their country," that it would be unthinkable for the executive or legislative branches to reject it. Once accepted, Jefferson wondered if the president and congress should "appeal to the nation" to approve it with a constitutional amendment.

Within a week, this intellectual debate came to an abrupt halt. Another midnight letter arrived from Robert R. Livingston with extremely alarming news: Napoleon "appears to wish the thing undone." The first consul was "basting" Finance Minister Marbois for committing 20 million francs to settle U.S. claims; Napoleon said the real figure was closer to four million. Bonaparte was also growling that if the bonds by which the U.S. government was to pay for Louisiana were not delivered within the specified time, "the treaty is void."

According to Livingston, the evil genius behind this sudden change in the dictator's mood was Talleyrand. The ex-bishop was making every imaginable "objection and insinuation" to change Bonaparte's mind. Livingston had no illusions about Talleyrand's motive. The foreign minister was furious at losing "the profits that might have resulted" if the negotiations had been left in his hands.

Another reason for Napoleon's unhappiness was the wrath of Spain, which accused the first consul of violating his solemn promise to King Carlos IV not to cede Louisiana to a third party. In another letter dated June 25, Livingston warned that "Spain is much dissatisfied," which, in turn, had made the French "sick of this bargain." They needed no more than the "slightest pretence" to abandon the treaty. The minister implored Jefferson to let "nothing prevent you from immediate ratification."

An agitated Jefferson dashed off a letter to Breckinridge, ordering him not to say a public word about a constitutional amendment because it might give France "a pretext for retracting." He rushed a similar letter to the cabinet, warning them that "the less we say about constitutional difficulties the better." Nevertheless, the president drew up another draft of a possible amendment, much shorter than his July version. It also divided the territory into white and

Indian sections. Again the cabinet told the president that an amendment, short or long, was not a good idea.

In an earlier debate on the subject, when Monroe was appointed envoy extraordinary and told to buy the Floridas, the cabinet members favored an opinion by Secretary of the Treasury Albert Gallatin. He maintained that the ability to acquire territory was implied in the Constitution by its granting the federal government the power to make treaties. This argument, based on an implied power, was straight Federalist doctrine that Jefferson found very hard to swallow.

In September the situation came to a boil of sorts when Senator Wilson Cary Nicholas of Virginia, the Jeffersonian majority leader in the Senate, begged the president to forget about an amendment. If he so much as mentioned it, Nicholas feared that the Old Republicans in the party's ranks would refuse to approve the treaty. Nicholas added that he personally saw nothing wrong with an argument based on the treaty-making power.

In a tormented reply, Jefferson admitted that Bonaparte could not be trusted and that ratification should be as swift as possible. But he still wanted an amendment of some sort, before or after the fact. He told Nicholas that the implied power interpretation reduced the Constitution to blank paper. Almost wistfully the president declared that he wanted to "set an example against broad construction" by appealing to the people for "new power." But if his friends thought otherwise, he would "acquiesce with satisfaction."

In fact, the president acquiesced with profound dissatisfaction. Jefferson realized that he was sacrificing his lofty—

and impractical—view of the federal constitution to the harsh necessity of power politics. He may well have sensed that in so doing, he was inflicting a wound on the strict-construction theory from which it would never recover.

In this same month of September 1803, the United States had to deal with the wrath of Spain, personified by the Marquis de Casa Yrujo, an ambassador who considered himself a personal friend of both the president and the secretary of state. He disturbed Madison's repose at Montpelier, his Virginia mansion, with a letter that declared the sale of Louisiana was a "manifest violation" of Spain's treaty with France and was therefore null and void.

Yrujo provided the secretary of state with a translation of the letter that the French ambassador to Madrid had sent to the Spanish secretary of state, dated July 22, 1802, when Louisiana was retroceded: "I am authorized to declare to you in the name of the First Consul that France will never alienate it."

When Madison returned to Washington in late September, he showed Yrujo's letter to Chargé Pichon. Madison suggested that Pichon write to Yrujo, who was still in Philadelphia with his wife's family, and ask him to sign certain papers that would be needed when Spain delivered Louisiana to the French prefect, Pierre Clement Laussat. The Spaniard flatly refused to sign anything. Instead he fired off another violent protest to Madison.

This time Yrujo claimed that Napoleon had failed to make good on his promise to persuade the powers of Europe to recognize King Carlos's son-in-law as the king of Etruria. Great Britain and Russia had declined to pay him this compliment. That meant Spain still owned Louisiana.

Pichon told Madison not to worry about Yrujo. He had been one of the most enthusiastic boosters of the transfer of Louisiana to France. He saw it as creating a strong buffer state that would keep greedy Americans from attacking Mexico and other parts of the expiring Spanish empire. Pichon, tattling on his ex-ally, told Madison that Yrujo boasted the cession would "strangle Hercules in the cradle."

Madison calmly refuted Yrujo's arguments. He quoted a letter from the Spanish foreign minister to Ambassador Charles Pinckney that clearly stated the province had been transferred to France. As for the recognition of the king of Etruria, Madison said that Spain may have this and other problems with France about the decision to sell, but there was no doubt whatsoever that France had the legal right to make the sale. Privately, the secretary of state said that Spanish objections were "too futile to weigh."

The most important result of this tempest in a diplomatic teapot was a cabinet meeting on October 4, at which President Jefferson asked his lieutenants if it would be advisable to take forcible possession of New Orleans if Spain refused to hand it over. The answer was a unanimous yes. The secretary of war, Henry Dearborn, was told to ready U.S. Army troops for this possibly unpleasant task. First, however, they had to surmount a barrier closer to home: persuading Congress to ratify the treaty and vote to appropriate the money to buy Louisiana's 838,000 square miles.

13
Triumph—and
New Perils

On October 17, 1803, a special session of Congress convened to hear President Jefferson's message about "matters of great public concernment." He began by recalling the "extraordinary agitation in the public mind" during the previous session of Congress over the Spanish suspension of the right of deposit in New Orleans. The chief executive claimed that the United States's "friendly and reasonable representations" had persuaded Spain to restore this right. But the problem of a foreign power controlling the mouth of the Mississippi meant "the danger to our peace would be perpetually exposed."

Therefore "propositions" had been advanced to obtain New Orleans and nearby territory. The "enlightened government of France," to whom the territory had been "restored," had responded to these propositions by deciding to sell the entire province of Louisiana in order to "permanently promote the peace, interests and friendship" of both countries.

Any resemblance between this description and the reality of the Louisiana Purchase was largely accidental. But Jefferson was not speaking as a historian. He was a president trying to persuade congressmen and senators who had spent the previous three months reading arguments pro and con about Louisiana in the newspapers. He expatiated on the value of the "uncontrolled navigation" of the Mississippi, the elimination of all "dangers to our peace," and the "fertility of the country." He described the acquisition as "an ample provision for our posterity" and "a wide spread for the blessings of freedom and equal laws."

Ultimately, Jefferson rested his case for the approval of the treaty on "the wisdom of Congress." He would rely on their counsel in occupying the territory, bringing the citizens of Louisiana into the Union, and dealing fairly with the Indians. These were the issues the president had tried to resolve in his drafts of a constitutional amendment. Not even a hint of that dangerous phrase was heard in the Capitol as the message was read.

Secretary of State Madison had rewritten Jefferson's draft of the message to minimize any and all difficulties with constitutional scruples. One provision of the treaty required that the United States continue to observe Spain's compacts with the Indians. This meant that a Roman Catholic priest would soon be on the federal payroll. Madison thought this sticky fact would be better mentioned when the administration got around to discussing new treaties with Indians, in the suitably distant future.

In the Senate, which had the constitutional responsibility for approving or rejecting the treaty, Majority Leader Wilson Cary Nicholas made sure there was virtually no debate. An attempt by the Federalists to demand all pertinent papers was brushed aside as unnecessary. Obviously briefed on the danger of a Napoleonic change of mind, the senators voted their approval the day after the treaty was submitted by an overwhelming 24–7. Not a single Republican defected and one Federalist senator, Jonathan Dayton of New Jersey, voted yea. Federalist Senator William Plumer of New Hampshire complained to his journal that his fellow solons "had taken less time to deliberate on this important treaty, than they allowed themselves on the most trivial Indian contract."

The president immediately exchanged the ratified treaty with the copy Chargé Pichon had received from Paris. The idealistic young Frenchman promptly forwarded to New Orleans the confirmation of the sale and orders to hand over the territory to the United States. Jefferson now submitted copies of the treaty to both houses of Congress so that they could vote on the next steps in the diplomatic process, in particular the $20 million that Napoleon Bonaparte was impatiently awaiting.

In the House of Representatives were many Old Republicans, and they proceeded to give Jefferson some palpitations. When New York Federalist Gaylord Griswold called for papers to prove that France, and not Spain, had a title to Louisiana, Majority Leader John Randolph tried to crush the request by an immediate vote. With a 3–1 Republican majority, he won by a mere two votes, 59–57. The next day Griswold was on the attack again, arguing that the territory could not be admitted without a constitutional amendment. In the ensuing debate, the Republicans sounded like Federalists, touting the implied powers of the government.

More threatening was the argument of Federalist Roger Griswold of Connecticut. He admitted that the Constitution's implied powers gave the government the authority to acquire Louisiana. But the Jeffersonians could not incorporate the people of the territory into the union, as the treaty required them to do. Louisiana could only be governed as a colony, the way the British ruled Jamaica or India.

Majority Leader Randolph scoffed at this argument and declared that the implied powers of the Constitution entitled the federal government to incorporate Great Britain or France into the union if the opportunity arose. With this all-but-total repudiation of strict construction, Randolph called for a vote on the treaty. The Republicans rediscovered party discipline and voted 90–25 to approve the treaty and appropriate the purchase price. No less than 17 of the 25 dissenting Federalists came from New England. For the moment, no one in the administration had the time or inclination to worry about this geographical fact.

The following week, the Senate debated the implementation of the treaty, exchanging similar arguments. The strongest Federalist statement came from dour, beaknosed Senator Timothy Pickering of Massachusetts, former secretary of state under President John Adams. He not only claimed that the Constitution gave Jefferson no power to incorporate Louisiana into the union but also insisted that the "assent of each individual state" was necessary, exactly as executives of a commercial company would insist that everyone approve a new partner. Other Federalist senators stoutly supported this contention, which was manifestly a political impossibility.

The Jeffersonians would soon discover the ominous implication of this argument. But for the moment, it was ignored by the Republican majority. They got their marching orders from Senator John Breckrenridge of Kentucky, who declared that if the treaty were rejected, the western states would secede from the Union and form a separate country. The Republican senators swallowed their doubts and approved the absorption of Louisiana into the union by an overwhelming 24–5.

To prove they meant business, the Jefferson administration also persuaded Congress to authorize the president to raise as many as eighty thousand men and allocated $1.5 million to cover the cost of this mobilization. Meanwhile, the president and his secretary of state had clerks at work feverishly copying the treaty and relevant documents for the takeover. Reports from New Orleans were making them nervous. The mostly French local population was reported to be unhappy about being sold en masse to the United States, and the Spanish were still saying that France had no right to sell the territory. It was not hard to imagine some hotheads fanning resentment into violent resistance—giving Napoleon a perfect excuse to void the deal.

The Jeffersonians prepared a proclamation aimed at dampening local enthusiasm for an uprising. It warned all and sundry that the "incivility" of Spain would not deter the United States from taking possession. "We shall retain our rights. But it belongs to you to decide whether you are disposed to share in them or attack them." As a carrot to this rhetorical stick, they described President Jefferson as "a philosopher who prefers justice to conquest" and urged them to make Louisiana "a garden of peace."

The president ordered Postmaster General Gideon Granger to get the documents certifying U.S. possession to New Orleans as rapidly as possible. Fresh horses were stationed every thirty miles and fresh riders every hundred miles to rush the papers to Natchez, where the army of occupation was assembling. Its paltry numbers—four hundred fifty regular troops plus five hundred mounted militia from Tennessee—somewhat deflated the tough talk of the proclamation. But Jefferson, still hoping for a peaceful occupation, left it up to Governor Claiborne and General Wilkinson to decide whether they needed the backing of six thousand militia that the governors of Tennessee, Kentucky, and Ohio had been told to assemble.

In early November the post riders began their marathon dash across a thousand miles of forest and stream to Natchez. For another seven weeks everyone in Washington, from the president to the lowliest government clerk, waited and wondered about what was happening in New Orleans. On Christmas Day, some of the suspense was broken by the news that the Spanish, thanks to a direct order from Madrid, had handed Louisiana over to the French on November 30.

Since Chargé Pichon's all-out cooperation had more or less guaranteed French compliance with the treaty, President Jefferson felt vastly relieved. But there would be no real end to the jangling mixture of hope and anxiety until he heard that the citizens of New Orleans had peaceably accepted Governor Claiborne and General Wilkinson and his troops.

While the Jeffersonians fretted in Washington, an earlier chapter in the story of Louisiana was drawing to a grim close on Santo Domingo. Until Napoleon declared war against England, General Donatien de Rochambeau seemed on his way to regaining control of the island. Reinforced by fifteen thousand men, he drove the black rebels from the chief seaports, cutting off most of their supply of guns and ammunition, and began launching devastating attacks into the interior.

When the news of the renewed war with France reached the Caribbean, the British West Indies fleet made Santo Domingo target number one. The royal navy bombarded the French-held seaports and smuggled guns and encouragement to the rebels. American merchants, with the tacit approval of the Jefferson administration, continued to supply the blacks with food and ammunition.

In August a desperate Rochambeau begged President Jefferson for a loan of $100,000 to save "the most beautiful possession of France." The response from Secretary of State Madison was silence. Soon the French were driven back to four ports, where they faced starvation and massacre. By October, Rochambeau was telling Chargé Louis Pichon that the situation could be rescued only if he received a million francs a month to buy food and ammunition. Once more Jefferson and Madison declined to help and U.S. bankers were equally cold.

In November 1803, Rochambeau, his ranks reduced to eight thousand men, retreated for a last stand in Cap Francois. With yellow fever continuing to ravage his ranks, the general signed an armistice with the rebels and surrendered his army to a British fleet cruising offshore. It was a humiliating end to Napoleon's dream of colonial glory.

In New Orleans, Prefect Pierre Clement Laussat issued a proclamation to the people, telling them that they would soon become U.S. citizens. The Frenchman said that the "advent of war" had been the reason for Napoleon's decision to sell Louisiana. He hailed the transaction as a "pledge of friendship" between the United States and France. He assured them that the first consul was still determined "to renew and perpetuate" the ties between Louisiana and France. He urged them to participate in U.S. politics and hoped they would become a "preponderating influence" in the U.S. government.

Laussat sent word to the Americans at Natchez that he was ready to hand over the province. General Wilkinson had visited New Orleans a few months earlier and knew that the Spanish garrison consisted of three hundred decrepit soldiers, half of whom on any given day were either ill or in prison. He advised Governor Claiborne that there was no need for the additional six thousand militia. The five hundred mounted Tennesseeans would do nicely as reserves. Leaving them behind in Natchez, Wilkinson and Claiborne led the four hundred fifty army regulars down the Mississippi in boats.

Wilkinson was looking forward to conferring with top Spanish officials in New Orleans. Madrid was almost $20,000 in arrears on their secret service payments to him. He saw the new situation created by Louisiana's purchase as ripe with potential profits. With the Americans a giant stride closer to the gold mines of Mexico, the dons should be eager to get advice and cooperation on how to keep the wild men of the West at bay.

There was no resistance when the Americans marched into the city. On December 20, at a ceremony in the riverside Place d'Armes, Laussat, flanked by Claiborne and Wilkinson, watched while the French tricolor was lowered and the American stars and stripes ascended the flagpole. Soldiers fired a volley in salute and cannons boomed on the river, where dozens of U.S. ships were anchored.

In the watching crowd there was not a trace of elation. A traveler from Paris described the scene: "An anxious silence reigned among all the spectators who flooded the plaza. When the flag reached the top of the pole, a cheer burst from a small group of Americans in the crowd." Their exultation made "more gloomy the silence and quietness of the rest of the crowd." Prefect Laussat shared the prevailing emotion. He burst into tears.

The good news reached Washington, D.C., on Sunday, January 14, 1804, in the hands of a member of Postmaster General Granger's early version of the pony express. Once more, President Jefferson made sure that the *National Intelligencer* got the information it needed for a front-page story. The next day, he sent a message to Congress announcing the final consummation of the great event. It was a veritable paean of presidential joy, ending with: "I offer to Congress and our country my sincere congratulations."

The Republicans wasted no time in making political capital of the triumph. "Never have mankind contemplated so great and important an accession of empire by means so pacific and just," declared the *National Intelligencer*. The paper published numerous fictionalized reports of how delighted the citizens of Louisiana were to become Americans. On Friday, January 26, the Republicans celebrated at a dinner for a hundred guests at Stelle's Hotel on Capitol Hill, with President Jefferson, Vice President Burr, and the cabinet as the guests of honor. Outside the doors, three cannons dragged from the Navy Yard on the Potomac thundered a salute. The guests entered to the resounding strains of "Jefferson's March," a new piece of music composed for the occasion. An ode in praise of the president was sung by several voices. Perhaps its most significant stanza was:

> To Jefferson, belov'd of Heav'n
> May golden peace be ever given.

After the president and vice president departed, a toast was offered to "the President of the United States." It was drunk with three hearty cheers. Someone proposed a toast to the vice president. There were no cheers and some Republicans declined to drink it. Aaron Burr's popularity in the Republican Party was continuing to decline.

Recently, he had gone to a Federalist dinner and offered a toast that quickly got into the newspapers: "To the Union of all honest men." Many people thought the vice president was preparing to launch himself as the leader of a third party that might attract moderate Federalists and national Republicans.

The vice president was pondering such a possibility. But it was only one among a number of options opened to him by the acquisition of Louisiana. Another course was suggested by the men around Senator Timothy Pickering, who considered the Louisiana Purchase tantamount to a rupture of the Union. When a Federalist senator from Connecticut told the vice president that New England planned to secede and form a separate nation, Burr did not say a word against the idea. In fact, he gave Senator Plumer of New Hampshire the impression "that he not only thought such an event would take place—but that he thought it was necessary it should."

Even more ominous was the stupendous preparations to invade England that Napoleon Bonaparte was undertaking in France. As the year 1804 began, the Man of Destiny was spending the United States's $15 million to assemble two hundred thousand men—designated "The Army of England"—in and around the port of Boulogne. Another army of workmen, many conscripted by Bonaparte's order, was building two thousand flatboats, each equipped with a cannon, that would carry this host across the English Channel. When his admirals told him that Boulogne was not big enough to launch the entire armada, Bonaparte put three thousand men to work dredging and enlarging the nearby fishing port of Ambleteuse so several hundred flatboats could sail from there on the same tide.

The rest of Europe watched in awe at the manic energy and enthusiasm that the first consul was inspiring in the French people with his vision of swift, total victory. This titan did not hesitate to alter the very geography of Europe's coast to achieve his goal! The disaster on Santo Domingo was as forgotten as the abandoned army of Egypt.

If Napoleon won this immense gamble and dictated peace in St. James's Palace to the humbled English, there was little doubt that the conqueror would soon find even more fault with the treaty that ceded Louisiana to the United States. He would have no difficulty persuading a terrified Spain to cede the Floridas to him. The United States, with no navy worth mentioning, would be unable to prevent him from shipping a hefty portion of the victorious army of England to this strategic territory.

With possession of two hundred miles of the east bank of the Mississippi, Bonaparte and his generals would soon close the river on some pretext, letting the Americans know who was in charge. Having the commander of the U.S. Army on the payroll of the Spanish secret service could only increase their confidence. If the United States chose war, the Bonaparteans would launch their veterans on a march of conquest from New Orleans to St. Louis to Montreal—where the liberation of the captive French of Canada would be celebrated. Talleyrand's wall of brass would appear along the Mississippi, and New France would become a menacing part of North America's destiny. As for President Thomas Jefferson's treaty purchasing Louisiana—it would be an amusing scrap of paper in the archives of the French empire.

14

Destiny Takes Charge

Continuing to celebrate the triumph of the purchase, in late January the Republicans staged a ball for five hundred people in Georgetown. Ladies wore their best finery, and gentlemen their red, green, or yellow waistcoats and silver buckled shoes. On the rear wall of the assembly room was an illuminated portrait of Thomas Jefferson framed by military banners.

The *National Intelligencer*, clinging to its faith in Republican simplicity, said the room's "plain unblemished walls" testified to the desire to avoid "spectacles that celebrate the achievements of warriors." With "Jefferson's March" at the victory dinner and this enshrinement at the victory ball, the Republicans were unquestionably out to elevate the president to the level of popular reverence accorded George Washington.

The Federalists declined to cooperate with this program. One of their disgruntled congressmen called the ball "the second act of the farce." In their newspapers, the Federalists concentrated on the way the Republicans had contradicted themselves by relying on the implied powers of the Constitution to justify the purchase. General Hamilton's *New York Evening Post* reported that during the debate over admitting the people of Louisiana to the Union, a "gentleman" had overheard two of Jefferson's cabinet members admit that this step was patently unconstitutional.

Jefferson did not help matters when he sent to Congress a hastily assembled farrago of information entitled "An Account of Louisiana" that cobbled together stories from Indians and wandering trappers and myths from speculative books, along with more reliable information. Among the wonders of the new territory was reported to be a mountain of salt on the upper reaches of the Missouri that was 145 miles long and 130 miles wide. There were also reports of Indians seven feet tall and herds of woolly mammoths with huge tusks.

The Federalists seized on these unlikely details and used them to ridicule the purchase and Jefferson as a gullible and unrealistic philosopher. William Coleman, editor of the *New York Evening Post*, wondered if along with the salt mountain there was also an "immense lake of molasses . . . and a vale of hasty pudding, stretching as far as the eye could reach." Other critics pointed out that the value of land in the eastern part of the country was certain to decline, once the law of supply and demand kicked in and people realized that there was virtually unlimited acreage awaiting them west of the Mississippi. New Englanders in particular predicted that Louisiana's vast reaches would lure people west rather than keep them in the East to work in the new factories that were rising.

The Federalist goal was to make Louisiana, especially the incorporation of its French citizens into the Union, look like an unconstitutional blunder. Underlying this line of attack was a continuing fear of the return of Napoleon, if he conquered England. The *New York Evening Post* thought Prefect Laussat's speech to the people of Louisiana was so important that it reprinted the text verbatim. The *Post*'s editor—and presumably the owner, General Hamilton—took special alarm at Laussat's claim that Napoleon intended to do everything in his power to maintain his ties with the Creoles, including his hope that they would become influential in the U.S. government. "Is there one man with a single drop of American blood in his veins whose pride is not aroused, whose prudence is not alarmed, whose indignation is not fired at this triumphant display of French arrogance?" asked the *Post*.

Laussat's statement that Napoleon's decision to sell Louisiana was forced by "the advent of war" with England enabled Hamilton and his alter ego, Coleman, to descant on how this proved that Jefferson's supposedly skillful diplomacy had nothing to do with the purchase. Here was an insider from France admitting that the whole thing was sheer accident.

The paper also attacked another clause in the treaty, which gave France and Spain most favored nation status in exporting goods to the United States for twelve years. The clause was certain to irritate the British, who were the dominant exporters to the United States. Worse, the $15 million paid to France would come from import duties. New England and New York, who did most of the importing, would pay for Louisiana while the South, which imported little, would gain most of the benefits from the territory, thanks to its proximity to their borders. The *Post* saw this as another example of Jefferson's pro-Southern, pro-French policy. The closer one studied it, the *Post* concluded, the more likely it became that the Louisiana Purchase would be "the greatest curse which ever befell this country."

That hyperbole reflected the letters that General Hamilton was getting from Senator Timothy Pickering and other New England Federalists, urging him to join their secessionist conspiracy. The plot was becoming more serious with every passing day. Senator Pickering, drawing on his experience as secretary of state, was planning to bring Great Britain into the game by offering London an alliance if they ceded Canada to New England to make a new nation in North America.

Vice President Burr remained a crucial player in this unfolding drama. The conspirators hoped he would not only enlist the support of New England Republicans but also might bring New York into the new confederacy. That would create a natural barrier along the Hudson River, making it difficult for an invading federal army to restore the Union. The opportunity for turning this vision into reality was the race for the governorship of the empire state in the spring of 1804. The Federalists urged Burr to run. They pledged him the support of their rank-and-file voters—and money to finance his campaign.

After a final attempt to achieve a rapprochement with Jefferson, which the president spurned, Burr decided to run for governor of New York. Only General Hamilton and a handful of his close friends opposed him. The Jeffersonian triumph in the midterm elections had more or less destroyed Hamilton's leadership in the party. His opposition to Burr was ascribed to jealousy.

Prominent Federalists such as Hamilton's brother-in-law, Stephen Van Rennselaer, a Hudson River manor lord wealthier than Robert R. Livingston, supported Burr. Even the editor of the *New York Evening Post* backed him. New England Federalists contributed money. In return, Burr all but guaranteed them that if he won, he would lead New York into the secessionist confederacy. He told Connecticut congressman Roger Griswold that the northern states "must be governed by Virginia—or govern Virginia."

Jefferson responded by offering the vice presidency to Governor George Clinton of New York, a not-so-subtle endorsement of the anti-Burr branch of the Republican Party in the empire state. Old and ill, the governor was no threat to Jefferson's plan to name James Madison as his successor in 1808. Clinton's followers, led by his nephew, DeWitt Clinton, the mayor of New York City, nominated Morgan Lewis, chief justice of the court of appeals, for governor to oppose Burr. They marshaled the formidable political machine that George Clinton had created in his almost continuous reign as the state's chief executive since 1777. A key player was James Cheetham, editor of the *American Citizen*, a newspaper totally controlled by Clintons.

During the campaign, Cheetham slandered Burr in almost every imaginable way. He published a derogatory letter that General Hamilton had written about Burr during the 1800 deadlock with Jefferson in the electoral college. When Burr declined to challenge Hamilton to a duel, Cheetham called him "the most mean and despicable bastard in the universe." He accused the vice president of stealing from the estate of a dead client, and of sadistically whipping American militiamen during the Revolutionary War. He described him as an atheist who mocked all religions, and an insatiable seducer who had ruined the reputations of dozens of respectable women in New York.

While Burr fought Jefferson and his surrogates for the future of North America, in Washington the president found himself threatened by war with Spain. Early in March, the Spanish ambassador, Marquis de Casa Yrujo, burst into Secretary of State James Madison's office and screamed abuse in his face. He was protesting the U.S. claim that the boundary of Louisiana included a large chunk of the east bank of the Mississippi in the Spanish colony of West Florida.

The administration based this claim on the maps and arguments that James Monroe and Robert R. Livingston had sent along with copies of the treaty. The Spanish, already paranoid about the aggressive Americans, grew frantic when Congress passed a bill at Jefferson's behest, creating a customs district in West Florida that included the port of Mobile.

Secretary of State Madison rushed letters to France, asking Monroe and Livingston to obtain French backing for their position. The envoys glumly reported that Napoleon's attitude toward the United States was declining into sullen hostility. The first consul blamed Jefferson and Madison for breaking the president's promise to support the army on Santo Domingo. A hefty percentage of the French people seemed to agree with him.

From the Caribbean came more evidence of French hostility. Many of the civil officials that Napoleon had sent to Santo Domingo fled to Cuba when Rochambeau surrendered his army. From this Spanish island they issued privateering commissions to ships from France and Spain, entitling them to seize any and all U.S. ships on the pretext that they were trading with the victorious black rebels on the island. The ships were brought into Cuban ports, where their cargoes were auctioned and their crews abandoned without money to buy even a mouthful of food.

In New Orleans, meanwhile, the new U.S. rulers were facing a hostile populace. Not a little of the enmity was generated by the government that President Jefferson had persuaded Congress to approve for the province. It contained not a trace of democracy. Every official, from the governor to judges, was appointed by the president. There was no provision for trial by jury. Jefferson had decided that the French Creoles lacked the education and experience to participate in democracy.

In Congress and in their newspapers, the Federalists roasted Jefferson for this "monarchical" government. Even some Republican congressmen were critical. One Pennsylvanian contemptuously described it as "royal." Another Old Republican compared Jefferson to Bonaparte. A Tennessee Republican admitted: "It really establishes a complete despotism."

Jefferson's congressional supporters angrily responded that the president was right. Principles of civil liberty could not "suddenly be engrafted" on people with no experience in self-rule. Many Republican congressmen claimed the Louisianians had no rights. They cited the way some had shed tears when the French flag was lowered and the Stars and Stripes replaced it. The House of Representatives voted its reluctant approval of the Louisiana government bill by a mere 6 votes, 51–45.

No one seemed to give any thought to the way the legislation violated the treaty with France, which had guaranteed the inhabitants all the rights of U.S. citizens. The Jeffersonians were giving Napoleon a perfect pretext to declare the sale of Louisiana invalid whenever it suited him.

Two other decrees from Washington, D.C., added to the spreading ire in New Orleans. The law setting up the authoritarian government voided all land grants after 1800 from Intendant Morales and other Spanish officials. The Spaniards had given away huge swaths of Louisiana to friends and relations when they heard that Spain had ceded the province to France. One of the larger beneficiaries was Edward Livingston, bankrupt brother of the minister. Losing this land only deepened his detestation of Thomas Jefferson.

The Federalists also assailed Louisiana because it would widen the number of states where slavery was legal. In response the Republicans had tacked a rider on the government bill forbidding the importation of slaves from abroad or from U.S. slave states, unless the blacks were brought to Louisiana by a bonafide immigrant to the territory. The Creoles claimed that this law made it impossible for them to expand and develop their lands.

Meanwhile, General Wilkinson, the commander in chief of the U.S. Army, was having treasonous conversations with Vicente Folch, the governor of West Florida. After many hours with the voluble general, Folch agreed to settle the problem of Wilkinson's back pay with a lump sum of $12,000 and to renew the annual stipend they began giving him in the 1790s. In return, Wilkinson advised the Spanish officials to defy U.S. attempts to claim that West Florida was part of Louisiana. He also urged them to arrest Meriwether Lewis and William Clark, who were in St. Louis, preparing to depart on their expedition. The Spanish took the first half of this advice but let the explorers march west unchallenged.

In France, during these same months, First Consul Bonaparte continued his manic preparations to invade England. He brushed aside warnings from his admirals that his flat-bottomed landing craft would be smashed to driftwood by the royal navy if British men-of-war caught them on the open sea. What if he lost twenty thousand men? said the Man of Destiny, who had sent fifty thousand men to their doom in fetid Santo Domingo. It would be a cheap price to pay for getting the rest of his two hundred thousand–man army on English soil. From the cliffs of Ambleteuse, the port he was enlarging, Napoleon wrote a friend in Paris: "I can clearly see the English coast. It [the channel] is a ditch one can jump whenever one is bold enough to try it."

Napoleon was encouraged by the panic raging in England. The government, after calling for three hundred thousand volunteers, revealed that it did not have enough guns to arm a third of them. The rest would have to rely on pikes. George III sought help from the Bishop of Worcester for a safe place to hide the crown jewels. Letters seized from captured British ships revealed a prevailing fear that if the French got ashore and proclaimed liberty, equality, and fraternity, the English masses would greet them as liberators. The *New York Evening Post* reported from a close reading of London newspapers that "the [English] public mind continues to be distracted."

The frantic British responded by trying to assassinate Napoleon. They put a band of sixty Bonaparte-haters ashore in Brittainy, led by a French general who had switched sides. French secret police soon scented the conspiracy and warned the first consul, who suspended the invasion program to launch a massive manhunt for his would-be killers. When they were captured, they named a co-conspirator, a relative of the executed Louis XVI, Louis-Antoine, the Duc d'Enghien. He was living just across the French border in the principality of Baden on money from the British secret service. He was supposed to come to Paris to ascend the French throne after Bonaparte's murder. The first consul seized the hapless Enghien and shot him at sunrise, outraging the crowned heads of Europe.

In New York, voters went to the polls at the end of April 1804, and Aaron Burr soon learned that he had been badly defeated. The *New York Evening Post* said the reason was "the very extraordinary attacks on his private character, which were circulated with an industry and an expence [sic] hitherto unexampled." James Cheetham gloated over this supposed triumph of Jeffersonian principles and added piously that Burr's defeat had rescued the United States from "a dissolution of the Union." He ranted about the way the New England papers were urging this idea.

The day before William Coleman published his sympathetic essay on Burr's defeat, he had reprinted an article from the Boston *Repertory* that laid out a series of arguments for dissolving the Union. The writer claimed that the chief purpose of the Louisiana Purchase was "the aggrandizement of the southern states and their accumulating power." There was only one solution to this threat: repeal of the provision in the Constitution that gave the South the right to elect a surplus of "white aristocrats" as representatives by counting as part of their population three-fifths of their black slaves. Since this repeal was never going to happen, the only hope was a "union" of the states north of Chesapeake Bay to regain control of their destiny.

Burr, now an odd man out in the brewing conspiracy, decided there was only one way to remain in the game. He had to eliminate General Alexander Hamilton from contention for the leadership of the new confederacy. On the basis of a remark Hamilton had made at a dinner party two-and-a-half months earlier, when he was actively opposing Burr, the vice president challenged the general to a duel.

The slur was mild compared to the abuse James Cheetham had heaped on Burr at DeWitt Clinton's orders and with President Jefferson's covert compliance. Hamilton could easily have dismissed his remark with a letter, denying that he meant anything personally dishonorable. But the code of honor that dominated politics in 1804 made a man who avoided a duel look like a coward.

General Hamilton, intimately acquainted with the likelihood of New England's secession, could not take the course of dishonor. Earlier he had issued a statement in the *Evening Post*, declaring that he would not hold public office again unless summoned to duty by a "civil or a foreign war." As he surveyed the political scene, the general feared that either might soon come to pass. He saw New England poised to secede, which made a civil war all too possible. If that conflict did not materialize, there was Napoleon, about to destroy England and turn his imperial attention to the Americans.

On the night before the duel, Hamilton wrote a letter to a leading New England Federalist, stating his final opinion of the plan to secede. "Dismemberment of our empire," he wrote, "will be a clear sacrifice of great positive advantages without any counterbalancing good." Why? Secession would not cure "our real disease; which is DEMOCRACY." Hamilton was remaining true to his original vision of the United States as a continental power—and revealing why he and his fellow Federalists were losing their contest with Thomas Jefferson's Republicans for control of this coming colossus.

Vice President Burr inflicted a mortal wound on General Hamilton with his first shot. The bullet inflicted equally mortal damage on the secessionist conspiracy. Federalists regarded Burr with loathing as Hamilton's murderer, disqualifying him for leadership in New England. With Hamilton literally dead and Burr politically dead, the conspiracy floundered to an embarrassed halt.

In Europe, the assassination plot left Napoleon in a distracted state of mind—so he claimed. Actually, he saw it as a perfect excuse to take the next step in his march to absolute power. He told his followers that as long as he held the precarious title of first consul for life he would have to fear such intrigues. Assassins would multiply because his death would leave no clear successor. The only way to discourage such a trend was for him to take the title of emperor of France and name a line of succession in his family.

The obedient Paris press immediately began telling its readers the importance of giving the Man of Destiny a crown. The yes-men who sat in the so-called legislative bodies hastened to add their approval, after extracting some supposed "rights" from the dictator. Next came another fake plebiscite, which approved Bonaparte's new status. The Corsican adventurer accepted the title of emperor of France on May 18, 1804.

After not a little arm twisting, Pope Pius VII agreed to come to Paris to crown the new monarch on December 2, 1804. At the climactic moment Napoleon seized the crown and put it on his own head, then took an oath to liberty and equality, leaving the pontiff humiliated.

In this charade, Napoleon managed to alienate almost everyone but his immediate followers. Any illusion that he represented the revolution vanished, both in France and in the United States. On the day of his coronation, the British government that had signed the Peace of Amiens fell, and William Pitt, the prime minister who had fought Revolutionary France in the previous decade, took charge.

Pitt immediately began rebuilding a coalition of Europe's royal powers. The murder of the Duc d'Enghien and the humiliation of the Pope inclined these rulers to listen to England's diplomats, especially when they dangled million-pound subsidies to sustain their armies. Napoleon further infuriated the Austrians by having himself crowned King of Italy on May 26, 1805. Soon French spies were reporting plans for an invasion of France from the east the moment Napoleon launched his army across the channel to demolish England.

Again postponing the invasion, Bonaparte marched his army of England east, throwing the members of the new coalition into confusion. The British, who could have put an army ashore and marched to Paris virtually unopposed, did nothing. In two stupendous battles at Ulm and Austerlitz, Napoleon smashed the armies of Russia and Austria and became the unquestioned, unchallengeable master of continental Europe. Grimly, with renewed confidence, he marched his men back to the channel coast to finish off his chief adversary.

By this time, however, Napoleon had been forced to admit that his flatboats could not survive in a rough sea, or in a contest with British men-of-war. With typical brutality he had launched dozens of them, loaded with soldiers and supplies, in heavy weather. Over five hundred men drowned before he was convinced that his matchstick fleet was folly. With Spain now in the war as an ally of France, Bonaparte decided to achieve naval supremacy by combining the French and Spanish fleets. As this unstable coalition headed for the English Channel, Admiral Horatio Nelson's British fleet intercepted it off Cape Trafalgar on the southwest coast of Spain on October 21, 1805, and demolished it.

The Man of Destiny had met his match. The gods of war had decreed he would never invade England. That meant a French fleet and army would never appear off the coast of Florida to menace Louisiana. The rest of Emperor Napoleon's sanguinary career would be devoted to war in Europe, until he met his ultimate defeat at Waterloo in 1815. By that time, Louisiana had long since vanished from his dreams of imperial glory.

15

The Final Challenge

In the fall of 1804 the American people, as distinguished from congressional orators and newspaper editors, had their chance to express their opinions about the Louisiana Purchase at the polls. Although Thomas Jefferson made no specific claim for credit—in those days, candidates for the presidency did not campaign personally—there was no doubt in anyone's mind that the purchase was the central act of his administration. Republican orators and newspaper editors did not hesitate to remind voters of its meaning.

Typical of this not-so-subtle electioneering was a celebration in New York on May 12, 1804, on the approximate first anniversary of the purchase. At sunrise, the same cannon in the fort on the Battery and on Governor's Island that had boomed in honor of James Monroe as he departed on his diplomatic journey to France now roared a "Grand National Salute." Every major building in the city hung out American flags and the ships in the harbor also hoisted the national colors. While church bells pealed, Mayor DeWitt Clinton organized a procession in City Hall Park.

Through the city streets marched a martial host, led by the commander of the city's numerous militia companies. He carried a white silk banner on which was inscribed: "Extension of the Empire of Freedom in the Peaceful, Honorable and Glorious Acquisition of the Immense and Fertile Region of Louisiana, December 20, 1803, 28th Year of American Independence, and in the Presidency of Thomas Jefferson."

Behind the uniformed marchers came the city's leading political organization, the Tammany Society, carrying a 15-foot-long white muslin map of the Mississippi River and the 838,000 square miles of Louisiana. The map was, of course, only an approximation of the geographical reality, but the applauding crowd of onlookers had no difficulty getting the central message.

That fall to no one's surprise, President Jefferson and his running mate, former governor of New York George Clinton, carried every state in the Union except Connecticut and Delaware. In the electoral college, the Jeffersonian team swamped the Federalist candidates, Charles Cotesworth Pinckney of South Carolina and Rufus King of New York, by a staggering 162–14. Even Massachusetts, the state that Senator Timothy Pickering had envisioned as the mainspring of his secessionist confederacy, succumbed to the magical sound of the Louisiana Purchase. In Congress, the Republican majorities remained proportionately huge.

Would anyone dare to defy such a mandate? The answer was a startling yes. In Louisiana, whose citizens could not participate in the election, dissatisfaction with the government that Jefferson had created for the territory remained intense. It was worsened by the ineptitude of William C. C. Claiborne, the man the president had chosen as the governor of the southern half of the territory. Unable to speak a word of French, he made no attempt to learn the language. He soon became convinced that he was surrounded by would-be insurrectionists and bombarded Jefferson with anxious letters. The citizens of New Orleans found his awkward, hostile style insufferable.

Claiborne's appointment was the result of the haste with which the Louisiana Purchase had been rammed through Congress. Jefferson originally planned to invite his and the United States' old friend, the Marquis de Lafayette, to govern the territory and serve as a bridge between the unhappy Creoles and the Americans. But there had been no time to dicker with Lafayette, or find anyone else of comparable prestige to take the job. Claiborne had been appointed instead, thanks to his proximity as governor of the Mississippi Territory—and his loyalty to Jefferson.

In December 1804 the Louisianans sent three delegates to Washington to demand a redress of their grievances. They carried with them a "remonstrance" written by Edward Livingston, the former mayor of New York, now a confirmed Jefferson-hater. The document was designed to embarrass the author of the Declaration of Independence. It asked why "political axioms" such as the right to vote and trial by jury became "problems" in Louisiana. The delegates demanded the rights guaranteed them in the treaty with France, including statehood. They threatened to take the first available ship to France and demand justice from Napoleon.

The Jeffersonians grudgingly admitted that the delegates had a case. With the president's reluctant approval, Congress passed an act on March 2, 1805, granting Louisiana an elective assembly of twenty-five members. They were also promised admission to the Union as a state when their population reached sixty-five thousand free inhabitants. But the ban on importing slaves and the refusal to honor any land grants from Intendant Morales remained in place.

The delegates professed severe dissatisfaction with these concessions and made no secret of it. One of the people who listened closely to their diatribes and expressed strong sympathy with them was the outgoing vice president, Aaron Burr. The delegates also told Burr about emissaries from Mexico who were walking the streets of New Orleans in search of support for a democratic revolution to free their country from the dead hand of Spain.

Discontent in Louisiana and unrest in Mexico fitted nicely into Burr's plans. As the British ambassador, Anthony Merry, explained to his government in a dispatch marked *most secret*, Burr had already approached him with a proposal to "effect a separation of the western part of the United States."

The unhappy natives of Louisiana could play a major role in this plan, which had the wholehearted cooperation of Burr's close friend, General James Wilkinson, the thoroughly corrupt commander in chief of the U.S. Army. All Burr needed to make it successful was a half-million dollars and the promise of a British squadron at the mouth of the Mississippi to close the river if the Americans tried to interfere with his western revolution.

Ambassador Merry thought the deal was a bargain. He pointed out that independent westerners would be a wonderful market for British goods, which could be imported from New Orleans and Canada. At the same time, the new nation would be unlikely to compete with the British merchant marine because they had only a single "bad port," New Orleans. Its inadequate harbor barred it from achieving the status of Boston or New York, whose ships were taking business away from British carriers at an ever-increasing rate.

Also in the game was the new French ambassador, General Louis Marie Turreau, a vulgar, swaggering man best known for the savagery with which he had smashed the 1794 counter-revolution in the Vendee region of France. General Bernadotte had been retained in France to help Napoleon win his victories at Ulm and Austerlitz. Turreau also became a public friend of the Louisiana deputies and was soon telling Tallleyrand that everyone in Washington expected the West to separate from the Union, under the leadership of Mr. Burr and General Wilkinson.

In the fall of 1805, Burr floated down the Mississippi and some of its tributaries in an elegant houseboat and received warm receptions from western leaders such as Andrew Jackson. All ardent duelists, they found no fault with the former vice president's dispatch of General Hamilton. Burr urged them to join him, not in a secessionist western confederacy but in an invasion of Texas, which would trigger a revolution in Mexico that would make them all rich. He expatiated on the timidity of the Jefferson administration, which was permitting the Spanish to bluff them out of West Florida.

The response was enthusiastic. To a man, westerners despised the effete "dons," and agreed that it was time to kick the Europeans off both the North and South American continents. They liked the idea that General Wilkinson was deep in the plot, ready to double-cross his Spanish paymasters and the Jefferson administration, and throw his regular troops into the rampage to gold and glory.

Burr was confident that the conquest of Texas and Mexico by an army of western adventurers would give him the money to create an empire in the heart of the continent. He, not Thomas Jefferson, would be the hero to whom the pugnacious westerners would turn. What exquisite revenge it would be, to take the Louisiana Purchase away from the hypocritical philosopher in the White House!

Several things went wrong with this Bonapartean dream. The British, fighting alone against Napoleon's "continental system," which barred British imports and threatened them with bankruptcy and starvation, were too harassed to embark on an adventure in the United States that would turn the Jefferson administration into their implacable enemies. Burr's friends and associates talked too freely about his plan and various newspaper editors, loyal to Jefferson, began printing alarming stories about the former vice president's intrigues.

Without British support, and with too much of the plan now public knowledge, General Wilkinson got a case of cold feet and itchy palms. He decided to betray Burr, which would earn him a bonus from his Spanish paymasters and make him a hero to President Jefferson. The general arrested the men Burr sent to New Orleans with ciphered letters, announcing that the great adventure was about to begin. Wilkinson rushed a wordy communique to the president, reporting a "deep, dark and widespread conspiracy" to start a war with Spain and revolutionize the western states.

An infuriated Jefferson issued a proclamation denouncing Burr and ordering his arrest, as well as the capture of the thousand-man force Burr had recruited in western Pennsylvania and Ohio. By the time Burr and his men reached Natchez, federal attorneys were armed with warrants and hundreds of militiamen wielded loaded guns that ingloriously ended the former vice president's febrile scheme.

In a sensational trial before the Federalist chief justice of the Supreme Court, John Marshall, Burr was acquitted because Marshall's political and personal detestation of Jefferson prompted him to bar most of the evidence. The government was unable to produce the constitutionally required two witnesses who saw Burr commit an overt act of treason, such as shooting or threatening to shoot a federal official. But Jefferson made sure that the evidence of Burr's conspiracy was published in dozens of Republican newspapers.

When leaders such as Andrew Jackson discovered that Burr's ultimate goal was the secession of the west, they too denounced him. Republican newspapers triumphantly proclaimed that the plot had failed because the West was "bigoted to Jefferson and liberty."

Easterners also responded with rage when they learned that a former high official of the government sought to deprive them of the bountiful acres of Louisiana. In

Baltimore, after his acquittal, Burr narrowly escaped hanging. Persona non grata everywhere in his own country, he fled abroad, where he spent the next five years vainly trying to persuade first the British and then the French government to finance his grandiose vision.

By the time a chastened Burr returned to the United States and obscurity in 1811, Louisiana was a permanent part of the country. The reports of the Lewis and Clark expedition had electrified the nation with descriptions of a region of broad rivers and rich soil, immense herds of buffalo and other game, and grassy prairies seemingly as illimitable as the ocean.

In January 1807, at an elegant dinner honoring Captain Lewis in Washington, D.C., the president and Congress hailed the success of the expedition. Joel Barlow, who had abandoned his Federalist New England roots to praise Jefferson and democracy, wrote a nine-stanza poem comparing Lewis to Columbus. The captain's "same soaring genius" had revealed "a new zone" in which humanity would prosper and thrive.

Louisiana's development could now be anticipated by Thomas Jefferson. "The world will see here such an extension of country under a free and moderate government as it has never yet seen," he said. "When we shall be full on this side [of the Mississippi] we may lay off a range of states on the Western bank from the head to the mouth, and so, range after range, advancing compactly as we multiply."

The president was relying on the "federal principle," designed by his brilliant partner, James Madison, in the Constitution. The union was capable of almost unlimited expansion, thanks to this unique mix of centralized and local government. It was this principle that enabled Jefferson to regard with equanimity America's ability to govern a nation of vast distances. From the Louisiana Purchase would come, in future decades, the states of Arkansas, Missouri, Iowa, Nebraska, South Dakota, almost all of Oklahoma and Kansas, and large portions of what is now North Dakota, Montana, Wyoming, Minnesota, Colorado, and Louisiana.

For the immediate future, by doubling the size of the United States, the purchase transformed it from a minor to a major world power. The emboldened Americans soon absorbed West and East Florida from enfeebled Spain, and fought mighty England to a bloody stalemate in the War of 1812. Looking westward, the orators of the 1840s who preached the "Manifest Destiny" of the United States to extend from sea to shining sea based their logic on the Louisiana Purchase.

Like many other major events in world history, the Purchase is a fascinating mix of destiny and individual energy and creativity. It would be unfair to deny the participants a significant role in the great milestone. Thomas Jefferson would have been less than human had he not claimed a major share of the credit. In a private letter to the liberal English scientist, Joseph Priestley, the president, reviving a favorite metaphor, said he "very early saw" that Louisiana was a "speck" that could turn into a "tornado." He added that the public never knew how near "this catastrophe was." But he decided to calm the hotheads of the West and "endure" Napoleon's aggression, betting that a war with

England would force Bonaparte to sell. This policy "saved us from the storm."

Omitted almost entirely from this account is the melodrama of the purchase, so crowded with "what-ifs" that might have changed the outcome—and the history of the world. Without Secretary of State James Madison's hardheaded realism about Santo Domingo, the French might have pressured Jefferson into keeping his promise to starve the black rebels into submission—and General Leclerc's army would have arrived in Louisiana more or less on schedule in 1802. Without Ambassador Robert R. Livingston's importunate diplomacy (to use Talleyrand's phrase), the French might have thought that they could manipulate the United States' attitude toward Spain's cession of Louisiana. Without Special Envoy James Monroe's willingness to risk bankruptcy and the wintry North Atlantic bearing Jefferson's ultimatum, Napoleon might have decided to take Talleyrand's advice and ignore the countless letters, memorials, and aggressive queries of the U.S. minister.

Also in the historical mix is that honest French republican, Chargé d'Affaires Louis Andre Pichon, who did not hesitate to tell his government the truth about the negative impact of their grandiose scheme on the U.S. government and its people. Even Talleyrand, the man who was least inclined to hear these home truths, admitted in a letter to Pichon at the close of his tour of the United States (which also ended his diplomatic career) that he appreciated the persistence and courage with which the chargé had told the truth.

Not to be forgotten is another French friend of the United States, Finance Minister Francois Barbe-Marbois. Toward the end of his long life, after being cashiered by Napoleon for being too honest, Marbois wrote a book about the sale of Louisiana, describing it as the crowning achievement of his career.

At least as important in the genesis of the great event were the black men and women of Santo Domingo. Their refusal to resubmit to the humiliations of slavery was a crucial factor in upending Napoleon Bonaparte's grand design. But it is doubtful if these black islanders could have sustained their resistance, even with aid from the United States, without the help of *Aedes aegypti*, those tiny female mosquitos with an evolutionary compulsion to feast on human blood and infect people with one of the world's deadliest diseases, yellow fever. With blind indifference these buzzing creatures destroyed General Leclerc's army.

Along with the sudden shift in the wind that rescued Robert R. Livingston from shipwreck and the ice that blocked General Victor's expedition, destiny has to be given its share of the credit for frustrating Bonaparte's vision of a militant New France manning the ramparts of Talleyrand's wall of brass in the Mississippi Valley.

Instead, destiny and the ongoing dynamism of the American Revolution combined to create an empire of liberty. With it came a new confidence in the United States' future in the hearts and minds of the heirs of the Revolution. The Louisiana Purchase created these epochal transformations. Today's Americans continue to be the beneficiaries of this providential turning point in the history of the republic.

Further Reading

Writing this complex story inevitably meant standing on the shoulders of earlier historians, who have explored it from many points of view. Perhaps the most engaging is George Dangerfield's biography, *Chancellor Robert R. Livingston of New York, 1745–1813* (1960). This warts-and-all portrait of the Hudson River grandee gives the reader a chance to experience the ups and downs of the Louisiana Purchase in its original, maddening contingency. For another important point of view, the fourth and fifth volumes of Dumas Malone's *Jefferson and His Time* (1948–1974) are also essential reading. Equally vital is Irving Brant's fourth volume of his biography *James Madison* (1941–1961). Also worth reading is Henry Ammon's *James Monroe: The Quest for National Identity* (1971). The same can be said for E. Wilson Lyon's *The Man Who Sold Louisiana: The Career of Francois Barbe-Marbois* (1942). Mr. Lyon also wrote another useful book, *Louisiana in French Diplomacy, 1759–1804* (1934). Enough books have been written on the man who really sold Louisiana to fill a good-sized library. I found Alan M. Schom's *Napoleon Bonaparte* (1997) especially helpful. On the magisterial side, but still eminently worth perusing in spite of its age, is Henry Adams's *History of the United States of America during the Administrations of Thomas Jefferson and James Madison* (1889–1891). Probably the best multifaceted recent treatment of the Purchase is Alexander DeConde's *This Affair of Louisiana* (1976). For those who don't have time to wade through *American State Papers, Class I, Foreign Relations* and *Annals of the Congress of the United States, 1789–1924*, a satisfying substitute may be Richard Skolnick's compilation from these and other original sources, *1803: Jefferson's Decision, the United States Purchases Louisiana* (1969).